Expert Advice From The Home Depot®

Bathroom
Design and Planning
1-2-3®

P9-DIY-433

Meredith BOOKS

Home Depot® Books
An imprint of Meredith® Books

Bathroom Design and Planning 1-2-3®
Senior Editor: John P. Holms
Art Director: Tom Wegner
Writers: Catherine Hamrick, Meg Goodman Richards
Contributing Writers: Cynthia Barnes, Linda Eggerss,
    Katie L. Smith,
Copy Chief: Terri Fredrickson
Copy and Production Editor: Victoria Forlini
Editorial Operations Manager: Karen Schirm
Managers, Book Production: Pam Kvitne,
Marjorie J. Schenkelberg, Rick von Holdt
Contributing Copy Editor: Kim Catanzarite, Julie Cahalan,
    Courtnay Wolf
Contributing Proofreaders: Janet Anderson, Kathi DiNicola,
    Heidi Johnson, David Krause, Sara Henderson,
    Gretchen Kauffman
Illustrator: Jim Swanson
Indexer: Donald Glassman
Electronic Production Coordinator: Mary Lee Gavin
Editorial and Design Assistants: Renee E. McAtee,
    Karen McFadden

Editorial and Design Contributions:
Abramowitz, Staub & Associates, Inc.
Designer: Tim Abramowitz
Editor: Catherine M. Staub

Meredith® Books
Editor in Chief: Linda Raglan Cunningham
Design Director: Matt Strelecki
Executive Editor, Gardening and Home Improvement:
    Benjamin W. Allen

Publisher: James D. Blume
Executive Director, Marketing: Jeffrey Myers
Executive Director, New Business Development: Todd M. Davis
Director, Sales-Home Depot: Robb Morris
Executive Director, Sales: Ken Zagor
Director, Operations: George A. Susral
Director, Production: Douglas M. Johnston
Business Director: Jim Leonard

Vice President and General Manager: Douglas J. Guendel

Meredith Publishing Group
President, Publishing Group: Stephen M. Lacy
Vice President-Publishing Director: Bob Mate

Meredith Corporation
Chairman and Chief Executive Officer: William T. Kerr

In Memoriam: E. T. Meredith III (1933-2003)

Photographers
Image Studios
Account Executive: Lisa Egan
Primary Photography: Bill Rein, Glen Hartjes, Dave Wallace
Contributing Photography: Dave Classon, Bill Kapinski, Shane Van
Boxtel, John von Dorn,
Remodeling Consultant: Rick Nadke
Assistants: Mike Clines, Roger Wilmers
Stylists: BJ Hill, Karla Kaphaem, Dawn Koehler

The Home Depot®
Licensing Specialist: Ilana Wilensky

Take our quick survey and enter to win a $1,000 gift card from The Home Depot®

Thank you for choosing this book! To serve you better, we'd like to know a little more about your interests. Please take a minute to fill out this survey and drop it in the mail. As an extra-special "thank-you" for your help, we'll enter your name into a drawing to win a $1,000 Home Depot Gift Card!

WIN THIS CARD!
OFFICIAL SWEEPSTAKES RULES AND ENTRY DETAILS ON BACK.
No purchase necessary to enter or win.

PLEASE MARK ONE CIRCLE PER LINE IN EACH OF THE NUMBERED COLUMNS BELOW WITH DARK PEN OR PENCIL:

1 My interest in the areas below is:

Cooking	High Interest	Average Interest	No Interest
Gourmet & Fine Foods	◯	◯	◯
Quick & Easy	◯	◯	◯
Healthy/Natural	◯	◯	◯

Decorating	High Interest	Average Interest	No Interest
Country	◯	◯	◯
Traditional	◯	◯	◯
Contemporary	◯	◯	◯

Do-It-Yourself	High Interest	Average Interest	No Interest
Home Repair	◯	◯	◯
Remodeling	◯	◯	◯
Home Decor	◯	◯	◯

(painting, wallpapering, window treatments, etc.)

Gardening	High Interest	Average Interest	No Interest
Flowers	◯	◯	◯
Vegetables	◯	◯	◯
Landscaping	◯	◯	◯

2 My plans to do a project in the following areas within the next 6 months are:

	High Interest	Average Interest	No Interest
Bathroom Remodel	◯	◯	◯
Kitchen Remodel	◯	◯	◯
Storage Project	◯	◯	◯
Plumbing	◯	◯	◯
Wiring	◯	◯	◯
Interior Painting	◯	◯	◯
Window Treatments	◯	◯	◯
Plant/Plan a Flower Garden	◯	◯	◯
Plant/Plan a Vegetable Garden	◯	◯	◯
Deck Building	◯	◯	◯
Patio Building	◯	◯	◯
Landscape Improvements	◯	◯	◯

3 I estimate that I have spent this amount of money on home improvement projects in the past 6 months:
Less than $1,000 ◯ $1,000-$2,500 ◯ $2,500-$5,000 ◯ $5,000-$10,000 ◯ $10,000 or more ◯

4 I purchased this book ◯   This book was a gift ◯

5 You *must* fill out all of the requested information below to enter to win a $1,000 Home Depot Gift Card.

Name: _____

Address: _____ Apt. or Suite # ____

Daytime telephone number: (____) ____

City: _____

State/Province: _____ Country: _____ Zip: _____

For D-I-Y trend research, please tell us your gender: Male ◯   Female ◯

Also, E-mail me with information of interest to me.

E-mail address: _____

Thank you for completing our survey! Please mail today to have your name entered to win a $1,000 Home Depot Gift Card. But hurry—one winner will be selected soon. See rules on back for entry deadline. To find more home improvement tips, visit www.homedepot.com or www.meredithbooks.com.

A. LETTERFOLD TOWARD BOTTOM OF SURVEY FORM, ALONG ORANGE TRIANGLES AT LEFT AND RIGHT.

B. MOISTEN BOTTOM STRIP, LETTERFOLD TOWARD TOP OF FORM, ALONG ORANGE TRIANGLES AT LEFT AND RIGHT.

BDP204

Take our quick survey and enter to win a $1,000 gift card from The Home Depot®

No postage necessary if mailed *inside* the United States.

If mailed *outside* of the United States, letterfold survey form, place in an envelope, stamp, and mail to:

Meredith Corporation
Home Depot 1-2-3 Books (LN-104)
1716 Locust Street
Des Moines, Iowa 50309-3023

Bathroom
Design and Planning
1-2-3®

Meredith®
BOOKS

Bathroom Design and Planning 1-2-3®

Table of Contents

Chapter 4
Shopping Guide **120**

Chapter 5
Fine Details **148**

Chapter 6
Universal Design **154**

Chapter 7
Remodeling Diaries **162**

How To Use This Book

Improving your bathroom is an investment in the equity of your home, your quality of life, and a reflection of your style and taste. Putting in a new bathroom can be one of the largest single expenses you will make, so whether you intend to do all or part of the work yourself or plan to use the services of an architect or designer and bring in a contractor to manage the entire job, you'll need some know-how and some good advice.

That's why the designers and associates at The Home Depot have put everything they know about designing and planning a new bathroom in one easy-to-use book. *Bathroom Design and Planning 1-2-3* will guide you step-by-step through the often complex and bewildering process of replacing, upgrading, or remodeling one of the busiest spaces in the modern home.

Take It Step-by-Step— ■ Design ■ Plan ■ Install

There are three distinct phases in any bathroom installation—creating a design, making a plan, and installing the components. How much time and effort is put into each phase will ultimately define how happy you'll be in your new bathroom. There aren't any shortcuts here. Every step is important.

A bathroom design that works is more than a floor plan and a lumber order; it's a package of information that will turn a dream into reality. A good design concept is a combination of style and function. It's the result of asking yourself the right questions; you can define not only your personal style and taste but also how you and your family

want to use the space now and in the future. A good design is all about the details. To get exactly what you want, you have to consider every element that will be part of your new bathroom including cabinets, countertops, plumbing and fixtures, floors, color, texture, lighting, surfaces, and window treatments.

A lot to think about? Absolutely. That's why you make a plan.

Make a Plan

The design concept will evolve into the plan for executing the installation. The plan will show you where the toilet and shower go, the color of the trim on the cabinets, and the specifications for the light above the vanity. It will ensure that you've complied with all the necessary building codes for safety before you begin tearing out the walls and prepare you for visits from the building inspector along the way. The plan will also reflect spatial and dimensional guidelines established by the NKBA (National Kitchen and Bath Association) for ease of use. And the plan—in the form of working drawings, layouts, and elevations—will become the ultimate authority for contractors, carpenters, plumbers, electricians, or anyone else you might have working on your project—including yourself. Finally, a solid and accurate plan allows you to create a realistic schedule for the work including lead time for ordering materials and the order of their installation. A plan will help you focus on the big picture when the old countertops and cabinets are piled in the garage, the house is draped in sheets of plastic, and the plumbing is only half-finished.

When you've completed the plan, you're ready to install the components.

Put It All Together

The first thing to remember is that no matter how well you've planned and how carefully you've scheduled, things are going to go wrong. You'll need a plan for solving problems as they come up. Some events will simply be out of your or your contractor's control—a shipping strike that delays delivery on the cabinets or the granite countertop cracked while it was being unloaded. Other things, such as accurate measurements, compliance with local codes, setting the right order of work, or well-defined contracts and work agreements, are definitely in your control. The bottom line is to control what you can so you can deal as effectively as possible with the issues you can't.

Find What You Need

The seven chapters of *Bathroom Design and Planning 1-2-3* are organized to provide you with a logical and easy-to-follow guide.

■ Important concepts are cross-referenced throughout the book.

■ Charts and checklists can be photocopied and filled out and filed to answer questions, solve problems, keep track of details, and evolve successful concepts.

■ Full-color photography and easy-to-understand illustrations clarify information at every stage of the process.

■ The combination of good design basics and practical advice makes a hard-working and concise reference on every aspect of designing and planning a bathroom.

In short, working your way through *Bathroom Design and Planning 1-2-3* is like sitting across the table from a designer who's making sure you've thought of everything.

Look Inside

Chapter One: Style and Function
Understanding the basics of design and how to turn theory into practice.

Chapter Two: Inspiring Designs
Applying design theory to nine basic bathroom shapes and styles.

Chapter Three: Planning
Defining your needs in order to draft layouts and floor plans and make decisions about what's going in the bathroom.

Chapter Four: Shopping Guide
Making informed buying decisions about cabinets, countertops, plumbing fixtures, lighting, flooring and more.

Chapter Five: Fine Details
Finding finishing touches that make your bathroom your own.

Chapter Six: Universal Design
Planning for ease of living and access—now and in the future.

Chapter Seven: Remodeling Diaries
Following three actual installations from the first design conferences to tightening the last cabinet knob.

working with THE PROS

If you're not doing the job all by yourself, you may have already thought about hiring a contractor, a carpenter, an electrician, or a plumber. You should also give some thought to working with someone who knows the whole process—a designer. Bathroom designers at The Home Depot—the people who helped write this book—are knee-deep in bathrooms every day. If you've got questions, they've got answers. They'll be the first to tell you that renovating a bathroom is a big job, but the results are well worth it.

In fact, most home centers have highly qualified designers on staff, and their services are usually free. When there's a charge, it's part of the package if the home center does the job. Other retailers—including cabinet shops—usually have a designer on staff who will work much the same way. You can also consult outside interior designers and architects. You wouldn't be shy about hiring an electrician. Don't be shy about working with a designer either.

CHAPTER 1

Style and Function

An attractive and well-planned bath follows guidelines for fixtures, storage, and counter space, as well as code requirements for venting, lighting, wiring, and plumbing.

Designing a successful bathroom means making the right decisions about everything from fixtures, faucets, and cabinetry to wall treatments and the style of flooring. The process involves planning, organization, scheduling, and dealing with the unexpected. The first step is creating a design that considers both style and function. The process is both creative and analytical and one in which you'll meet challenges and create solutions step-by-step.

CHAPTER 1 CONTENTS

left Increasingly, a master bathroom is seen as a place to escape daily pressures, relax, and unwind. Fixtures that once were considered luxuries such as whirlpool baths are becoming essential parts of a modern bathroom.

Style

Many people tend to think of style as it refers to popular themes in decorating such as country, Tuscan, Asian, traditional, French provincial, or contemporary. Style, when referred to in design, also defines a group of concepts (sometimes called principles) that help you make decisions about the look and feel of a room. The goal of the process is to create a bathroom that will accurately reflect your personal style and taste.

On the following pages you will learn about the basics of style and design—including color, texture, shape, line, form, pattern, detail, scale, proportion, unity, variety, balance, rhythm, and emphasis—and how each principle will affect the final design of your kitchen. In the second section of this chapter, you'll explore how to make your ideas functional. In the chapters that follow, you'll take what you've learned about style and function and apply them to planning the bathroom of your dreams.

above This contemporary wall-hung sink is all about style and all about function too. The single-handle lever is easy to operate. There is ample room on the edge to hold soap and toiletries, and the chrome towel rod is within easy reach.

Understanding Color

Working with color is one of the most pleasurable aspects of decorating. Color is a powerful element in design, setting a room's tone and affecting mood and emotion.

Warm colors such as red and orange convey cheer and liveliness, like a crackling fire. Yellow, a happy color, evokes a sunny day or daffodils bobbing in early spring. In northern climates or in rooms facing north, homeowners often incorporate warm colors as a counterpoint to cool temperatures and indirect sun. In contrast, cool colors communicate calm. The greens of leaves and grasses are restful. You may associate a blue sea with calm and

a faraway purple mountain with dignity. Cool-color rooms facing south or in a hot climate appear to diminish heat. That's why you often see blues and greens in beach houses.

Color also affects how you perceive a space. Warm colors seem closer than they really are, whereas cool colors recede. For example, a dark red ceiling appears to be lower than if it were painted pale blue. An oak bookcase stands out against (or seems to advance from) a pale green wall. However, against a dark tan wall, it blends in. Use warm colors to make a room cozy and soft, and cool, light colors to open up space.

The Color Wheel

Understanding color involves more than noticing its impact on your perception. The color wheel, which organizes the visible spectrum of colors and shows the relationships between them, is a useful tool in developing a color scheme.

There are 12 pure colors, those that have not been mixed with white or black, on the most commonly used color wheel.

Primary colors—red, yellow, and blue—are equidistant from each other on the color wheel. Of all colors, they are the brightest. They cannot be created from any other colors.

Secondary colors—orange, green, and violet—are derived from mixing equal parts of the primary colors. Red and yellow yields orange; yellow and blue, green; blue and red, violet.

Tertiary colors result from mixing an equal part of one primary and its adjacent secondary color: red-orange, red-violet, yellow-orange, yellow-green, blue-green, and blue-violet.

The 12 pure colors are rarely used in interior decorating except for emphasis. They are too strong, or intense. Black and white are not colors—at least technically. However, they are used to make shades and tints of colors. Tone is how light or dark a color is.

Adding white to a pure color diminishes its intensity, producing tints, or lighter versions, of that color. The more white that is used, the lighter the tint. (To make pastels, start with white and tint it with other colors.)

Mixing a pure color with black also reduces intensity and produces shades, or darker versions of the color. Mixing black with white produces gray.

Hue refers to the undiluted color from which a tint or shade is derived. The primary, secondary, and tertiary pure colors of the color wheel are all hues, as are the infinite number of colors that result from mixing them together. A color may have a wide range of tints and shades, but they all share the same hue.

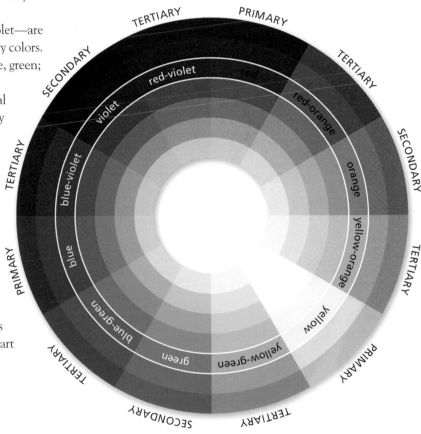

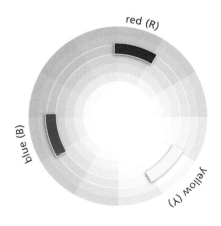

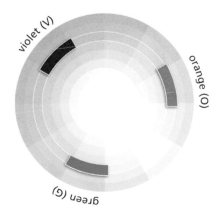

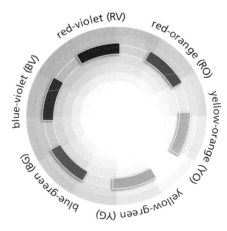

3 PRIMARY pure colors

3 SECONDARY pure colors

6 TERTIARY pure colors

Color and Light

Different types of lighting, as well as the amount, affect color. When making decisions about color, test swatches or paint chips in the actual space and under the lighting conditions in which the colors will be used.

Compared to sunlight, incandescent light makes objects appear redder and warmer; reducing the amount of light with a dimmer enhances the effect. Fluorescent light, typically cooler than sunlight, makes colors seem washed out. To counteract this cold effect, install lamps that approximate daylight or select warm colors for the room. Look for bulb types designated daylight or warm white.

When testing color samples, also bear in mind that color becomes stronger as it covers more area. For example, the red on a small paint chip becomes stronger on a wall.

The color wheel comes in handy when you're planning a color scheme for your bathroom. These basic schemes, which illustrate color harmony, will get you started.

Color Schemes

Monochromatic Colors

A monochromatic scheme uses the tints and shades of a single color. For example, look at a color card from a paint center; it shows paint chips in a range of tints and shades for one color. A single-color scheme is a nice approach if you seek a serene or simple bathroom. Begin by selecting a single color; then add interest by mixing in that color's shades and tints. The darker and lighter hues keep the eye moving, preventing boredom.

In a monochromatic scheme, a combination of three different tones generally works. The space needs deep-colored areas, midtones, and highlights. For instance, to create a successful all-white scheme, pick a yellow-tinted (versus a blue- or gray-tinted) white paint for the overall room color. The yellow tinting imparts a warm look, like a slightly aged patina. For the trim you might choose creamy white. For surfaces, such as flooring and countertops, avoid sterile white and choose materials that are warm white.

The more contrast between the tones, the more energy a room exudes. The subtler the tones, the more quiet the mood.

above This slice of the color wheel shows all the tints of yellow-orange. Combining these tints and shades will create a monochromatic color scheme.

left A monochromatic color scheme doesn't mean a lack of color options.

Analogous Colors

Analogous colors are neighbors on the color wheel. Although rich, an analogous scheme is soothing. If you start with blue as a foundation, you might pull in adjacent colors from the wheel, such as purple and green. For layered interest, blend in tones of the intermediate colors of blue-purple and blue-green. The trick is to allow one color to dominate the combination. Study the color wheel to come up with other analogous color schemes, such as red-orange-yellow or orange-yellow-green.

above Textures and tints of yellow and yellow-green create a color palette of depth and contrast.

left This section of the color wheel shows all the tints and shades of yellow and yellow-green, creating an analogous color scheme.

Complementary Colors

A complementary scheme incorporates opposite colors—such as violet and yellow, red and green, and orange and blue—on the color wheel. These combinations energize a space. Rooms in which a lot of activity occurs, such as master or kids' bathrooms, are candidates for a complementary scheme. The trick to a complementary scheme is allowing one color to take center stage. Weave its counterpart color into the setting with fabric, trim, or accessories. Use complementary hues of the same intensity.

above A pleasing blend of complementary colors is evident in this subtle red and green scheme.

left The color wheel shows all tints and shades of red and green, creating a complementary color scheme.

Analogous Colors with Complementary Accents

Analogous colors with complementary accents make a pleasing color scheme. An example would include orange, yellow-orange, and the complementary color blue-violet. To lower the intensity of this combination, use tints and shades. Place complementary accents in several strategic locations or use an accent as a single focal point.

above The strong colors in this scheme prove an agreeable and pleasing combination.

right These sections of the color wheel show all tints of orange, yellow-orange, and blue-violet, creating an analogous scheme with complementary accents.

Triadic Colors

A triadic color scheme uses three colors equidistant from one another on the color wheel. The primary colors of red, blue, and yellow are an example. Combining the secondary colors of orange, green, and violet is another. Achieving a triadic scheme is challenging. Such a combination usually requires moderation by using tints or shades instead of pure colors. You can control this vibrant scheme by limiting it to a small area and using it in concert with a neutral color, such as white.

above A triadic scheme offers drama even when the tints and shades are subtle. Also try combining pure colors.

right These sections of the color wheel show all the tints and shades of yellow-orange, blue-green, and red-violet, creating a triadic color scheme.

left Classic black and white marble tiles installed on the diagonal lead the eye across the foyer into a formal powder room. Using black tiles across the threshold creates a transition between the two spaces. The straight vertical lines of the doorway frame the oval mirror and enhance the symmetry created by the wall sconces and the fixture handles on the graceful pedestal sink. Squares in the wallpaper pattern echo the checkerboard pattern on the floor.

Line, Shape, and Form

A room is made up of different lines, such as the edges of a countertop or where the floor and wall meet, each of which leaves an impression. The vertical lines of a column communicate stability. The horizontal lines of a floor or ceiling suggest rest. A diagonal line, such as the slant of a ceiling, creates a sense of movement. The curved line of a countertop that follows the shape of an oval sink seems softer or less rigid than a right angle formed by horizontal and vertical lines.

Lines create interest and contribute to the style of a room. However, overuse can distract. Too many diagonal lines, for instance, force too much movement into a space.

The eye also is drawn to simple, complete geometric shapes such as circles, squares, rectangles, and triangles. In contrast, incomplete shapes create tension. You may see these shapes in the planes that make up walls, the floor, the ceiling, and countertops. Rectangular shapes often dominate a room. A room is most pleasing when the shapes are harmonious.

You also can discern shape based on where objects are placed. For instance, part of a large master bath may be divided into two areas—one as a dressing area and the other as a sitting area with a fireplace and two soft, deep chairs or a chaise lounge.

Form plays a part in furniture as well. For example, clean, minimal shapes characterize furniture that dates from the late 1920s until the early 1960s. Conversely, deep, cushy chairs used for casual seating do not have such crisp outlines. Whatever its form, furniture needs to be functional, and that means comfortable.

right Mixing different textures of stone creates visual excitement in this tiled shower enclosure. The small, roughly shaped tiles that make up the terrazzo floor add color and the uniform, rectangular shapes of the bench and wall tiles provide stability and a sense of formality.

above The stuccolike faux treatment of the walls adds depth and density, giving this bathroom wall an old-world feeling.

right The iridescence and softness of the weave in this shower curtain balance nicely with the texture of the tiles.

Texture

The actual or perceived texture of a surface or object adds interest to an overall decorating scheme. In a monochromatic setting, various textures take on a major role. In the absence of different colors, woven or nubby window treatments or small accent pieces, such as baskets or carved candlesticks, break up an otherwise plain landscape.

Texture comes mostly in the form of surfaces in the bath. Cabinets may be smooth laminate or beaded board. A countertop may be granite or a smooth, solid surfacing. A floor may be ceramic tile or hardwood. A decorative

finish, such as combing, gives a wall visual texture while hiding imperfections.

Match textures to the mood of the room. Textured surfaces are used in casual settings. A painting technique such as fresco may give a powder room an old-world feel. People often equate smooth, shiny surfaces with a contemporary look.

Texture also is linked with acoustics. Soft textures such as carpet absorb sound, whereas hard, smooth textures such as tile do not.

Pattern

Pattern occurs when a motif is repeated. Like texture, pattern adds interest. In a bath, different surfaces offer plenty of opportunities to use pattern. A wall might sport hand-painted decorative tiles or different-color tiles in a planned arrangement. Pattern in flooring varies widely.

You can use uniform ceramic tiles or a mix of large and small tiles. You can select from many patterned wallcoverings (as long as they're moisture-proof) or stencil a pattern on walls.

Pattern also changes how space is perceived. For example, vertical stripes make a surface appear taller and narrower, whereas horizontal stripes make it appear lower.

Pairing a single pattern with a solid color is always safe but may be dull. Mix patterns for effect. To ensure harmony, use patterns that share a common texture, color, or motif.

below right   Dark fluid veins in these marble walls create a flowing and elegantly formal pattern.

below   Multiple patterns, such as the horizontal tongue-and-groove ceiling and the paneled doors, create movement in this bathroom.

below   Laying tiles in opposing patterns creates obvious transitions between rooms. The colors of the tiles and the grout are compatible, but the patterns enforce a sense of movement.

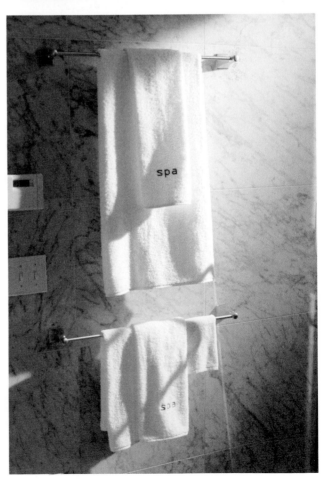

Detail

Details such as cabinet knobs and handles, trim and molding, or the right wall sconce or pendent light are the kinds of finishing touches that add depth and dimension to a bathroom. Hardware, accessories, and lighting fixtures are major factors in defining style. These important finishing touches should be chosen as carefully as the more obvious parts of a bathroom, such as vanity cabinetry, plumbing fixtures, or bathtubs. A well-chosen towel bar or toothbrush holder supports the overall bathroom design.

Details emphasize shape and line and help focus attention on major design elements. Add interest by accenting larger forms or lines to help define the style of the room.

Well-chosen details need not be small. Vanity mirrors encased in the proper frame define style. Details can be functional as well as decorative. An intricately patterned ceramic tile floor is easy to maintain and adds beauty as an important design element. Carefully chosen details will truly distinguish any bathroom.

above Considering the number of cabinet knobs and drawer pulls that are present in most bathrooms, it's easy to see why choosing the right ones is such an important decision.

above right and below right Matching brass gooseneck fixtures create pleasing symmetry and reflective elegance. The use of multiple mirrors for the vanity is an almost sculptural detail.

below Wall sconces come in many shapes and sizes and offer such a variety of functions that selecting the right ones can take time. Try different fixtures in the bathroom until you find the ones that suit the design.

Scale and Proportion

When you place elements in your bath that are appropriate to the size of the space, you achieve proper scale and proportion. When these elements of design are not applied, the design disturbs rather than pleases. For example, a small storage shelf seems insignificant in a grand master bath just as an oversize whirlpool tub might overwhelm a more modest bath. A heavy light fixture hung above a small wall-mounted sink in a powder room feels oppressive just as a large mirror over a small vanity looks weighty.

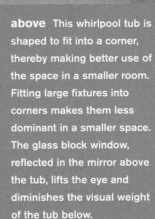

above This whirlpool tub is shaped to fit into a corner, thereby making better use of the space in a smaller room. Fitting large fixtures into corners makes them less dominant in a smaller space. The glass block window, reflected in the mirror above the tub, lifts the eye and diminishes the visual weight of the tub below.

left The ornate bowl sink, along with its fixture and the massive vanity mirror with the light above, would be visually overwhelming without the density and strong vertical rise of the combination linen and display cabinets on each side. Granite wall tiles are used to frame and scale the strong visual elements of this traditionally elegant vanity sink area. A larger lighting fixture above the sink would improve visibility at the mirror.

Unity and Variety

As an element of design, unity means harmony—experiencing parts of design as a whole rather than individually. For example, similar patterns or related colors create unity. Variety—expressed in different shapes, textures, or colors— keeps unity from becoming monotonous.

left The unifying element in this bathroom is the wainscoting which frames the shapes and varying scales of the sink and toilet. The horizontal lines in the woven window shade create visual variety when juxtaposed with the vertical lines of the wainscoting panels.

Balance

There are two basic means of achieving visual balance—symmetry and asymmetry.

Symmetry is the most recognized type of balance. Forms of equal size and visual weight are arranged on each side of an imaginary center line. They mirror one another, communicating formality and stability. A fireplace flanked by bookcases or windows is a classic example.

Asymmetry creates visual balance by properly juxtaposing objects that vary in shape, size, and color. Asymmetry communicates openness and informality. Many bathrooms are structurally asymmetrical because the placement of doors, windows, and cabinets on opposite walls does not share the exact configuration, though the elements may be of equal visual weight.

above Asymmetry is expressed on the glass counter of this towel rack by juxtaposing shapes and colors. The towels are hung symmetrically below.

left Symmetry is evident in the columns that flank the platform bathtub, the wall sconces, and the window on the rear wall which creates a center line. A single vase on the left step and greenery above right lend a hint of asymmetry to this arts and craft bathroom.

Rhythm and Emphasis

When you think of rhythm, music comes to mind. Rhythm varies in music; it may be simple or complex. Think of visual rhythm as a steady pattern of elements that visually connect. An interruption of color, lighting, or objects keeps the pattern from becoming tiresome.

Emphasis occurs when one element takes on more importance than others. For example, a dressy powder room may have a mirror embellished to make it stand out. A sizable freestanding claw-foot tub beneath a bay window draws attention in a master bath.

right A checkerboard pattern on the ceiling of this powder room relates rhythmically to the larger diamond pattern on the floor. The checkerboard pattern is repeated in the skylight, emphasizing the slope of the ceiling and drawing the eye upward and outside.

what level of REMODELING?

The least expensive category in bath **remodeling** is a facelift, or cosmetic redo. This typically involves installing new surfaces (floors, countertops, etc.) and possibly replacing some fixtures.

A **general renovation** can range from a major cosmetic redo to a fairly substantial construction project, such as changing the layout, adding new windows, carving out a privacy compartment, or making other structural changes within the existing space.

Another category is an **expansion.** In some cases, a renovation accomplishes a lot, but you may need more space—which means cutting into a bedroom, closet, or hallway. A variation on this is the bump-out, which often involves pushing out a window to create the perfect spot for a large tub or shower. Consider this option when you talk with building professionals. Many

bump-outs do not require a foundation and cost less than true additions.

Another option is **conversion,** that is, adapting another space in your home into a bath or building a completely new addition. A good place to start is a laundry or utility room, because plumbing lines are already in place. If you look to an attic or basement space, you usually can cut costs by stacking a bathroom over or under an existing bath.

You may start planning an expansion and somewhere along the way realize that with careful planning, a simple change in your layout will accomplish your goals at a much lower cost. Or you may think you want to rip out everything and start over, but after doing your research, you realize that tiling the floor and adding a skylight will achieve a satisfying change.

Function

All designers need to think about practical details when creating a great bathroom. Brainstorming about style is fun, but if a beautiful bathroom possesses style and doesn't function efficiently, it's a waste of time and money. The bathroom can be a reminder of what might have been if the proper attention had been paid to function.

A functional bathroom evolves from an organized process of reviewing practical considerations, such as placement of sinks, toilets, showers, and bathtubs. Other important considerations are fixtures, mirrors, lighting, ventilation, surface treatments, and flooring.

Because bathrooms are such busy places, it's also necessary to consider patterns of use by family members so that the space can be zoned effectively to ensure privacy, comfort, and safety.

use your RESOURCES

Return to these pages on functionality and use them as references and resources as you finalize the plans for your new bathroom. They will be especially useful as you review the planning section in Chapter 3 and the shopping guide in Chapter 4.

above Nowhere in the home do style and function come together more apparently than in the family bathroom. A rain shower not only gets you clean, it relaxes you at the same time. Good bathroom design combines both practicality and beauty, offering ease of use, reliability, and comfort.

right Creating a separate enclosure for the toilet allows privacy in the most open bathroom plan. Privacy is an essential consideration, especially when several family members will use the bathroom at the same time.

Basic Bathroom Layouts

The way you use your bath dictates which category it falls under. The major categories include master baths, family baths, children's baths, guest baths, and powder rooms or half baths. Variations exist within each major category.

Baths have three activity areas: the toilet, the sink, and the bathing area, which could include a shower or tub. All baths have a toilet and sink. Those that serve as general-purpose or family baths also feature either a tub or shower or both.

Master Bath

In today's world, a master bath is a place to relax.

Most master baths have a vanity with two sinks, a shower, a separate tub, a toilet, and adequate storage. In addition, many incorporate extras such as a whirlpool tub, a sauna, a steam shower, and a bidet. Larger bathrooms are divided into zones to offer increased privacy.

Some master baths boast a quiet, comfy place to read, listen to music, or escape the hurry and rush of the day. Master baths often add other special amenities to enhance a sense of luxury and to add convenience.

Here are some features to consider for a master bath:

- Fireplace
- Media area
- Speakers in the ceiling
- Shower sound system
- Sit-down dressing area
- Mini workstation: small table, chair, and telephone
- Snack station or kitchenette
- Coffeemaker

Less conventional solutions work well in many cases. Consider designing a separate powder room in the master suite, freeing up more open space for bathing, grooming, and dressing in the main area of the bath. Or if you prefer the privacy of a smaller bath, you can remodel to provide two separate baths off the master bedroom.

below Serenity and calm are the order of the day in this intimate and comfortable master bath. The monochromatic color scheme in muted greens invites relaxation.

above A large walk-in closet just off the bathroom makes dressing easy. More shelving on the wall would add extra storage. Master baths are often a series of smaller rooms connected as a private suite.

Family Bath

A family or general-purpose bath is most conveniently located near the bedrooms of the family members it is intended to serve. Design it to accommodate and offer privacy to several family members, who often need to use the different zones at the same time.

A common strategy is to place the bathtub/shower and the toilet in one zone and leave the sink and vanity area in another. Using pocket doors adds to the compact efficiency of the design by creating privacy without having to provide clearance space for the opening and closing of the doors. Provide adequate lighting and storage space in each of the various zones.

If you have adequate floor space in your family bath, consider the following features:

- A large double-sink vanity so that two family members can wash up and groom simultaneously
- Separate shower and tub fixtures
- Plenty of storage space
- Extra towel racks and hooks
- Adequate clear floor space

above Two sinks and an abundance of storage allow multiple family members to use the space. Adequate storage keeps bathroom clutter to a minimum.

In smaller spaces, you can install a tub/shower combination. Another space-saving idea is to use recessed shelving and smaller fixtures. Some cabinetry also has built-in fold-down tables or shelves that serve as work surfaces when needed.

Children's Bath

For baths specifically geared to one or more children, keep in mind some additional needs. Consider dropping the level of the vanity by an inch or two. It's also a good idea to include some hooks for towels, which are easier for most kids to reach than racks or rods. When designing a bath for your kids, remember that they will grow and change. Today it may be helpful to have a built-in bench in the tub. However, the 9-year-old who resists a bath at every turn will soon turn into a teen who practically lives in the shower.

If you have adequate space, an arrangement that works well with two children is the Jack-and-Jill layout, which typically has two separate sink/toilet areas with a shared tub/shower zone in the center. One variation places sinks on either side with a shared toilet and shower zone in the middle; another features one side with a toilet, sink, and tub, and the other with a toilet, sink, and shower. Any arrangement that gives your children some privacy will be greatly appreciated as they grow.

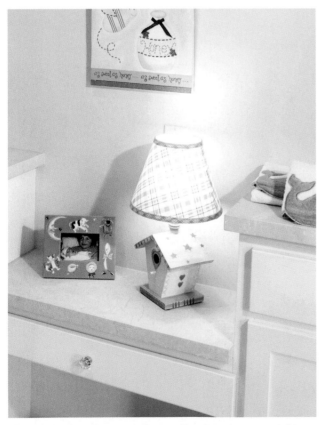

above Bright but easy on the eye, the dressing area of this children's bath is perfect for a youngster. As children grow older, change color schemes and accents to accommodate changing tastes.

Powder Room

A powder room, also commonly referred to as a half bath, is often located on the main floor and is used by guests.

If you have a true powder room, that is, a bath that has limited use, you can splurge on finer materials that might not be practical or economical in heavy-traffic baths. With limited space, stylish and practical design options include a pedestal sink, a corner sink and vanity, and using high-end materials for the fixtures and surfaces.

For privacy's sake, the optimal layout for a powder room allows for an entrance or transition area. If space does not permit, have the powder room open into a hallway or secluded area rather than directly into a major living area. Try to include at least minimal storage. Don't forget to install an adequate ventilation system.

Consider your lifestyle when designing your powder room. In many homes, the downstairs half bath gets heavy traffic from family members, visiting children, neighbors, and other guests. If this is the case, you can still go for a stylish and practical design, but you may want to modify your selection of preferred materials.

left **This powder room is designed in a simply accessorized country style. It is comfortable but functional and invites guests to step inside for a moment of privacy.**

Guest Bath

Options abound for a bath designed to accommodate overnight guests. If you have space for a separate guest bath, put yourself in the visitors' shoes and incorporate special touches that will provide your guests with the sense of being in a home away from home.

If your guests will have to share your bath, consider designing a master bath with a private opening from the bedroom and a second opening from the hall for guests. Include a partition, such as a sliding frosted glass partition or pocket door, which offers the option of closing off one sink and toilet to create a powder room for guests.

Some homes have space for what is often referred to as a three-quarter bath, which has a sink, toilet, and stand-alone shower but no tub. Not only an excellent choice for a guest or spare bath, it may also work well for teenagers.

Sometimes a downstairs bath serves multiple functions as a powder room, a guest bath, and if you include a door to the outside, a mudroom of sorts. The latter is an excellent option to consider if you have a swimming pool.

above **A guest bathroom doesn't need all the amenities of a master or family bath, but it should serve the basic needs of a visitor in a stylish and tasteful manner.**

CHAPTER 2

Inspiring Designs

Your dream bathroom starts with personal inspiration and becomes a reality by searching out concrete ideas. Applying the principles of style and function, and giving consideration to the details, provides you with limitless possibilities.

A perfect bathroom serves the needs of everyone using it. Whatever style and size bathroom you choose, it must work as part of the overall design of your house and it should complement the rooms that surround it.

On the following pages you'll explore nine bathrooms to help you find the inspiration for your own design solutions. Each of these bathrooms is a balance of style and function—they are beautiful, and they work.

CHAPTER 2 CONTENTS

left Increasingly, baths are seen as a place to escape daily pressures and unwind. In this bath, high polish marble, sleek black surfaces, and white cabinets represent the height of elegance. Whether you seek continental luxury or improved storage in a family bath, explore this chapter to find beautiful and practical ideas to jump-start your planning.

Measuring 15×15 feet, this bathroom is large but stunningly simple, with a garden tub as its focal point. Durable and waterproof, travertine stone is used on the vanity countertops and the large tub surround.

Tranquil
Escape

Architectural simplicity, neutral tones, soft lighting, and a whirlpool tub render a peaceful setting.

With a whirlpool tub, a soothing spa experience can be created in a master bathroom. Water circulation—usually by jets and hoses built into the wall of the unit—creates the action.

Whirlpools range in material and price. The least expensive type has a gel coating sprayed or painted onto a mold. Large units, such as tub/shower combinations, are often gel-coated. Gel coating is porous, so the tub will collect dirt and lose its shine more quickly than nonporous acrylic tubs.

Like a gel-coated tub, an acrylic unit is reinforced with fiberglass. However, it is more durable because it starts out as one thick sheet that is formed into the shape of the tub. A cast-iron unit with an enameled surface is the strongest material, although its weight poses a potential problem. The bathroom floor must be able to support it, and installation can be costly. Acrylic and gel-coated tubs allow for built-in features, such as curved armrests and shelves, and feel warmer to the skin than cast iron.

A whirlpool has a motor, so sound is a concern. Gel-coated and acrylic tubs absorb more noise than cast-iron units.

Whirlpool Weigh-In

The 15×15-foot bathroom featured here is large enough to accommodate a large whirlpool. Homeowners with less space can find smaller models, such as standard 5- or 6-foot-long alcove sizes. Styles also vary, from corner units to deck-mounted and freestanding tubs. Anyone considering a whirlpool needs to bear in mind not only the weight on the floor but also the physical challenge of getting the tub into the house.

Consulting a plumber to ensure the capacity of the water heater can meet the demand of the tub is a wise move. For example, a 40-gallon water heater cannot serve a 99-gallon capacity tub. Electrical requirements should be considered as well. To operate, each pump needs a separate circuit or electrical service. Larger tubs may have two or more pumps.

above Angled in the corner, the tub has a sculptural look—an ideal foil to the bath's sharp lines. There is plenty of room for two. A seat allows the user to ease into the water.

left Recessed halo downlights augment the natural light filtering through a large window made of glass block cubes. If there's no time for a long soak, the homeowner can duck into the adjacent shower. The ceiling over the bath and shower was box framed to handle electrical fixtures, to insulate, and to modernize the look. Plexiglass storage units hold toiletries while adding aesthetic interest.

left The stone slab around the tub also extends into the shower area, functioning as a ledge for seating.

below and right The toilet is separated from the rest of the bathroom. The arrangement of the toiletries on the towel rack adds dimension.

above Surrounded by clear tempered glass, the walk-in shower adds to the room's light, airy look.

below and right Above each sink is a set of folding mirrors that expand and extend to provide a range of magnifications. The round mirror and sink contrast with the rectangular vanity for a pleasing geometric effect. The white cabinets offer ample storage to ensure an uncluttered look.

right The sinks (and tub) are adorned with polished chrome faucets that deliver a sheet of water cascading over a wide, flat surface.

above This platform whirlpool tub fits neatly into a corner and is big enough for two to take a comfortable soak.

Dry-Tub Test

Just as you would test a mattress by lying down on it in a showroom, don't hesitate to sit in a whirlpool tub. It's the best way to see how different models fit your body. Ask about additional features such as a safety mechanism in the water return. In some models, the system turns off if an object, such as a washcloth or a child's toy, blocks the return. If you like to use bath oils, gels, or other scented products, check with the dealer about any restrictions.

Many circulating whirlpool systems do not tolerate such products. And remember that some maintenance besides regular surface cleaning is necessary. The circulation system must be cleaned of residue periodically (monthly to once every three months, depending on the model). This usually entails adding detergent, operating the tub, and then flushing it with clean water.

left A waterfall spout sends water cascading gently into the tub. The effect is not only visually pleasing but appealing to the ear as well.

This bath is designed so that the two athletic homeowners can simultaneously unwind after a workout. The roomy shower offers an invigorating spray, while the jetted tub is the perfect place to relieve sore muscles.

Contemporary Curves

Other master baths may boast more space, but this room measures up, thanks to smart planning.

The layout of this bath ensures that certain amenities tuck in neatly in a limited space. The rounded, custom-built shower, inspired by a visit to a kitchen and bath showroom, is definitely a showpiece, anchoring one end of the rectangular room. Spacious enough for two adults, it is constructed of gray ceramic tile. A shower curtain and liner, hung on two rods made of brushed nickel, enhance the soft look.

A privacy compartment would make the bath appear smaller, so the toilet is situated in a corner and discreetly concealed by a partial wall. One shower wall helps enclose the area. Across from the double vanity, a recessed whirlpool tub fits into another corner.

Large mirrors above the sinks and tub, as well as two windows, reinforce openness. The color palette—gray, dove, soft white, and honey tones—creates a calming atmosphere. Spending enough time with color options before you make final decisions about the color scheme is one of the most important design steps in the process.

Tile Talk

Using the same ceramic tile throughout the bath creates harmony. However, the varying sizes and shapes—square tiles on the shower walls and larger rectangular ones on the floor and tub surround—prevent monotony. Flooring tiles can be used on bathroom walls by using special trim finish pieces.

Ceramic tile is waterproof, durable, and easy to maintain. As a surface material for a tub or shower surround, it must be applied on top of water-resistant wall material such as cement backerboard which is durable and water-resistant. Although more expensive, cement-board ensures that your bathroom is waterproof, not just water-resistant.

Tile does not stain easily, but grout does. For easy maintenance, the homeowners chose a dark grout. They also opted for a shower curtain, not only for its soft effect but also because a glass door would require frequent cleaning.

below The stain of the hallway door matches that of the birch double vanity. Ceramic floors can be chilly, so a small heater inset at the base of the vanity keeps feet warm on winter mornings.

above This shower is a welcome sight at the end of a wearying day. In this case, a shower curtain is a wise alternative to a door, which would require custom-fitting.

Vanity Warm-Up

As a counterpoint to the gray tile, the vanity cabinetry is birch. Specially mixing several stains produced its reddish honey-blond tint. The spacious countertop boasts double sinks, with a window and an expanse of gray tile separating the two. The striking sink fixtures, which match those of the tub, stand up to the visual weight of the sinks. Like the faucet, the easy-to-grasp rounded handles are set on substantial pyramid-shaped bases. Large mirrors and two three-bulb vanity fixtures offer excellent visibility for shaving or applying makeup. In keeping with the simple design, the window treatment is a pleated shade.

above The curvy overhang of the two sinks gives the counter visual clout by echoing the shape of the shower. The vanity is higher so that the tall homeowners do not have to stoop. The size also allows more undercounter storage for towels and toiletries. The standard vanity height is about 31 inches without the countertop. Some manufacturers offer special cabinets about 33 inches high for user comfort.

above True beauty is in details. The warm tones of the birch vanity subtly repeat in the copper swirls that highlight the gray ceramic tile of the shower stall and floor.

Terrific Tub

The large jetted tub is recessed with a graceful, curved apron. A convenient separate spray attachment makes for easy shampooing without using the shower. The tub is contoured for comfort.

top The luxury of a jetted bath and shower is undeniable. However, double-use bathrooms may require extra mechanical or natural ventilation and a larger water heater. On-demand heating systems, which deliver hot water as needed, are wise solutions for double-use bathrooms.

above The fixture for the jetted tub matches the fixtures on the sinks.

Jet SET

Ideally, jets should be adjustable in direction and force. Some need to be positioned to reach parts of the body that get sore after a long day—the lower back or feet, for example.

Partial Wall

A partial wall next to the shower discreetly shields the toilet from the rest of the room and provides a convenient shelf for displaying lush foliage as well as housing for the switches that control the room's lighting fixtures. The toilet is a shade called tender gray that echoes the soft dove shade of the walls. This understated hue provides a harmonizing link between the bath's elements. It also casts a calming effect over the entire room.

Details

above Decorative mirrors hung horizontally on the wall in the toilet enclosure reflect houseplants displayed on the partial wall that offer a degree of privacy.

below left A brushed metal towel ring by the vanity sink adds both convenience and a decorative detail.

below Two three-bulb vanity fixtures and domed lights in the shower and toilet area light the room.

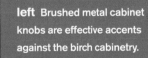

left Brushed metal cabinet knobs are effective accents against the birch cabinetry.

left Concealed hinges on the frameless cabinetry allow the doors to mesh seamlessly when closed. The hinges are fully adjustable to ensure the doors hang squarely and evenly.

Because space is usually limited in a powder room, carefully choose the elements that will go into it. Especially striking objects, such as an ornate mirror or an unusual lighting fixture, should become the focal point in the room. Space may be limited, but when designing your powder room, allow your imagination to soar.

Power-Up Powder Rooms

Powder rooms are potential jewels that lend themselves perfectly to personal expression. Creating a new powder room is an inviting opportunity to free your imagination.

Whether tucked away under a staircase, off the front door, or added to the end of a long hallway, powder rooms are private spaces in public areas that are gaining popularity. They are especially popular with families who entertain frequently or simply enjoy the convenience of a bathroom facility close to the main activity centers in their homes.

Powder rooms also create an opportunity to have some design fun by incorporating unusual features, such as specialty sinks and cabinetry, or by using color in ways that might not be appropriate in the rest of the home. The scale of a powder room, which is usually small, means careful selection of toilet and sink but lends itself to experimentation and personal statement. Consider wallpaper, faux painting techniques, striking mirrors and accessories, and interesting floor treatments. Incorporate shelving or display space for unusual objects and artwork.

Show off your sense of design by turning a simple room into a unique showcase of your personal style and taste.

Location

What a powder room lacks in space, it makes up for in convenience, especially when you have company. A half bath on the main floor truly pays off during morning rush hours. Whether adding on a powder room or working within an existing space, it's important to consider several key points: location, size, door, fixtures, lighting, wallcoverings, and floor coverings.

Privacy Is Important

When it comes to location, you need to give thought to available space, convenience, and privacy. The most practical and least expensive solution is to place the powder room directly above or below an existing bath and connect directly into existing plumbing. If that's not an option, consider an entry hall or a location off the kitchen—near but not right off the dining room or living room (to ensure privacy). You also can convert a utility closet or the space under a staircase into a powder room as long as there is adequate headroom.

Building codes require sufficient ventilation, which means you must provide an operable window or an exhaust fan that is vented through an external wall or the ceiling.

Doors

If space is particularly limited, install a door that swings out of the powder room instead of into it. A door that opens into a small bath cuts down on available space and makes entering and leaving awkward. A door that swings in also might impede reaching someone who needs assistance in case of an illness or accident. If the walls will accommodate pocket doors, they are a good solution in limited spaces. Opt for a high-quality sliding mechanism because repairs can be difficult. Pocket doors also tend to be less soundproof than swinging doors.

above The warm glow cast by the fixture above the mirror invites guests into this powder room conveniently located off the kitchen.

above The simple design of this pedestal sink with its softly rounded lines offers a strong contrast to the traditional and more formal decorative finish on the walls and the ornate vanity mirror with shaded lamps above. Mixing styles in small spaces is often a means of creating visual interest.

Basins

Pedestal sinks are popular choices for powder rooms because of space restrictions. But if there's room for a vanity, a wide variety of basin options is available that will suit any design scheme or budget and add a little flair and focus along the way.

Choices range from simple, smooth, and clean to more ornate sculpted models. Hand-painted or patterned basins fit well in traditional or country styles and offer a distinctive and custom look.

Hand-painted decorative basin

Smooth and contemporary

Sculpted basin

Patterned oval basin

Layout

Because the space allotted for a powder room is usually tight and often irregular in shape, placement of the sink and toilet will take some thought. Ideal clearances are not always possible, but you should play with the floor plan until you achieve the best fit possible.

below left and below right Both layouts shown here make maximum use of available space and still allow some room for decorative details. Focal points such as an appropriate pedestal sink are important elements in small spaces.

Fixtures

Invest most of your budget in the toilet and sink. The powder room is for guests, so many people like to splurge on quality construction, durable finishes, and high-end models. Some homeowners opt for a dressy look by installing vanities that look like furniture—warm, dark wood; fine finishes; and details. If your powder room is a tight fit, a pedestal sink or a wall-mount sink is a smart choice.

Incorporate counter space if possible. Guests need a place to set cosmetics, purses, or other personal items. An alternative solution is to build recessed shelves into a wall between studs; the resulting niche is decorative and functional and doesn't take up valuable floor space.

above The half-wall creates a private zone for the toilet and blocks a view of the toilet from the entryway. The wood trim and molding illustrate how details give the powder room a finished look.

above The one-piece toilet, with an elongated bowl, is a more expensive option but has a streamlined look in this small space. These toilets are cast as a single piece and are easier to install and clean. Accessories are minimal but effective. The iron plant stand pairs nicely with the framed print above the toilet.

size MATTERS

A basic powder room with a standard-size toilet and small wall-mount sink tucks into as little as 12 to 13 square feet, but you'll probably want something roomier. To figure out size, determine how much space you require between fixtures. Some powder rooms have 30 inches of width devoted to the toilet (15 inches from the center of the toilet in both directions) and 21 to 27 inches between the toilet and the sink. If your floor plan allows, you can leave 36 to 42 inches for the toilet and 30 to 36 inches between the toilet and sink.

above Pedestal sinks are space-savers and offer a sleek contrast to other elements such as vanity mirrors, textured walls, and flooring.

above Pedestal and console sinks create focus in a powder room. They are available in various styles to complement any decor.

above Guests will appreciate the generous glass-top counter, which offers ample room for purses, cosmetics, jewelry, and other personal items.

above The exposed drainpipes are streamlined so as not to distract from the overall design. The molded decorative edge around the shelf announces its presence and adds an ornate touch.

Bathroom Design and Planning **43**

Mirrors and Lighting

The size and shape of the mirror above the sink depends on personal taste. If your powder room has strong vertical lines, a round or unusual shape softens the look. A mirror spanning the width or height of one wall makes the space appear larger.

Ideally a powder room has three lighting zones: overall, mirror, and over-the-shoulder. Lighting a mirror on three sides with Hollywood-type fixtures renders a flattering reflection. A pair of sconces on either side of the mirror and a light in the ceiling also work well. A single light produces shadow and is not sufficient.

above This ornate mirror is outfitted with lights on either side, ensuring minimal shadow.

below This three-light fixture provides adequate illumination for guests to refresh themselves. The mirror reveals a linen closet.

above With its ornate scallops and leaves, the mirror is a focal point. In an artful mixing of materials, the nickel light fixture and sink fixtures are a counterpoint to the mirror's gold finish.

above left and right A decorative planter adds dimension to the walls. With flowers painted the same color as the wall, this decorative towel holder combines form and function.

Details

Small decorative touches—a stylish soap dish, a wall-mounted planter, a towel bar or ring, a tissue dispenser, and a wastebasket—have a big hand in creating a finished look. You can dress up a powder room that has a furnished look by adding columns, turned legs, spindles, corbels, brackets, toe-kicks, and moldings.

above Mixing shapes, sizes, and colors of granite floor tiles creates strong visual movement. Carrying the tile up the wall acts as a unifying element. Light-colored grout emphasizes the variance in shape and color.

above A freestanding wood cabinet reflects the trend toward using furniturelike cabinets and vanities in powder rooms and other baths. The use of wood brings warmth to the room and is an interesting contrast to a sink and countertop. The bottom sections of the cabinet (not shown) provide storage space, a true luxury for a powder room. The top shelves, outfitted with frosted-glass front panels, provide an area to display collectibles.

left and above left Matching brushed nickel sink fixtures and accessories create a sense of continuity in this small space.

Dramatic and elegant, this three-quarter bath serves as both a welcoming guest bath when overnight guests call and as a private bath for one of the family's three children.

Family
Drama

When the homeowners were ready to remodel a dated 1960s bathroom, they looked to their children for inspiration.

This dramatic three-quarter bath functions both as a guest bath when overnight visitors call and as a private bathroom for one of the family's three children. The newly remodeled bath updates a 1960s room that featured peeling wallpaper and a trickling toilet and had no vent fan or duct work.

The homeowners knew the redesigned bath would have to withstand daily use by a child, and still be inviting for overnight guests. Though the bathroom is small, a smart layout creates space for a shower, allowing the room to function as a hardworking family bath. During the remodeling project, the homeowners removed the tiles and wallpaper that dated the room. They rebuilt a partially rotted wall, adding heating and cooling vents for year-round comfort. A new sink and toilet combined with new lighting, wall color, and window treatments complete the transformation from dated to dramatic.

Dramatic Color

Looking at the vibrant red walls in the newly remodeled bath, it's hard to imagine that the homeowners were originally conservative with color. When they first moved into their home, the homeowners stuck to what they thought were safe off-white walls throughout the house. But those plain walls were a perfect canvas for the couple's children—budding young artists with access to crayons. When the original wallpaper in the bath began to peel from the humidity, assisted by small fingers, the homeowners knew a dark dramatic paint color was the way to go. The dark color hides fingerprints and doesn't encourage crayon drawings—and it provides a dramatic backdrop for new white fixtures and neutral tiles. To select the wall color, the homeowners welcomed the advice of an interior designer who looked to the rooms near the bath for further inspiration. The nearby family room has sage walls and a sofa with cranberry accents. The designer recommended the same cranberry tone as the color for the bath. Though bold, the color palette is simple, using only two colors: cranberry and white. The floor and shower tiles are neutral, with warm undertones that highlight the wall color.

above The curved edges of the light fixture, oval mirror, and oval sink basin work together to provide a unified look for the vanity area and soften the room's otherwise sharp lines.

above Softly draped fabric used as a valance is elegant and creates a sense of movement in the room. The muted cranberry tones in the fabric coordinate with the bold tone of the walls. A simple roller shade is dressed up with fringe and delicate fabric to suit the style of this bath.

above The polished chrome faucet complements the sophisticated look of the bath.

above A three-bulb fixture provides ample crosslighting in this small bath because the light fixture is wider than the mirror. Crosslighting eliminates shadows that form when the area in front of a mirror is not evenly lit.

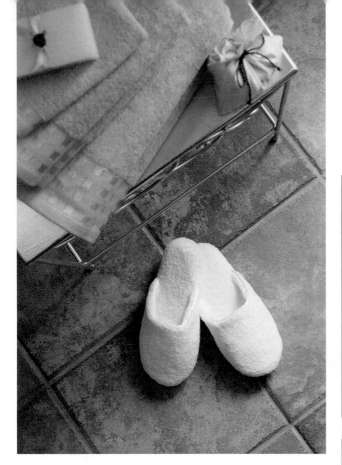

left Tile floors are a great choice for bathrooms—water resistant and easy to clean. Select a tile with a matte or textured finish. Avoid glossy tiles, as they can be slippery when wet.

Hardworking Design

Planning for the years when each of their three children wants ample private bathroom time, the homeowners carefully planned this bathroom space to incorporate a three-quarter bath with sink, toilet, and stand-alone shower. Space necessitated a pedestal sink so the homeowners selected one with flat space around the bowl to hold bathroom essentials and grooming items. They chose matte-finish ceramic tiles that stand up well to the splashed water and traffic of a hardworking family bath.

above Mixing sizes of tiles in the shower creates visual interest without overpowering the room or competing with the bold red walls.

left Pedestal sinks with a wide rim are good choices for small bathrooms, providing space for necessities such as soap, toothbrush, and toothpaste.

This sleek retro bathroom offers high style with crisp black and white tiles, and glass, chrome, and white fixtures. Small touches of red serve as an accent color.

Retro
Revival

The clean, simple lines and crisp black and white color scheme of this small bath are in keeping with the style of the 1930s home.

When the owners of a 1930s home decided to remodel their guest bathroom, they quickly determined that a retro Art Deco-inspired bath would be most in keeping with their home's style. The clean, streamlined fixtures that complement Art Deco also make the most of the available floor space in this full (4'10" × 9'4") bathroom.

When selecting fixtures for a small bath, consider the difference in size between several styles of sinks and toilets. Even minimal differences in the dimensions of a pedestal sink, for example, can make a dramatic difference in how the fixtures fit in a small bathroom, and how open the space appears. Because this bathroom is used primarily for guests, the homeowners also gained space by eliminating some storage. A simple glass shelf above the sink, and a painted wood shelf with a towel bar near the mirror, provide nicely for visitors.

Art Deco Design Elements

For the remodel, the homeowners utilized design elements characteristic of the Art Deco style popular in the 1920s and '30s when this home was built. These features include simple lines, geometric design, contrasts in color, and chrome and glass accessories. The black and white tiles, for example, create a geometric pattern on the floor. A variety of tile sizes and shapes—from 3×6-inch brick wall tiles to 6×6-inch square floor tiles accented with 2×2-inch black tiles—provide interest without breaking from the simple, streamlined design approach. Chrome and glass fixtures throughout the bath are functional and stylish, and in keeping with the period style.

above Slim-line fixtures make the most of a small bathroom and free up floor space, preventing the bathroom from feeling cramped. Touches of red dress up the black and white color scheme.

left Toilet paper holders can be utilitarian and stylish. This one is from the same design line as the other fixtures and coordinates with the entire decorating scheme.

above The glass and chrome mirror and shelf match the faucet, toilet paper holder, and toilet from the same line. Gently curving fixtures reinforce the retro style of the bathroom, and fit well in the small space.

left Accessories don't always have to be functional; often they can be purely decorative. This life-sized penguin stands alertly by the shower as if preparing for a swim. An occasional touch of humor can aid in creating an inviting environment.

left The elegant profile of this small chrome faucet pairs perfectly with the trim pedestal sink in this Art Deco design. Polished chrome is easy to clean and doesn't oxidize, so it will remain attractive.

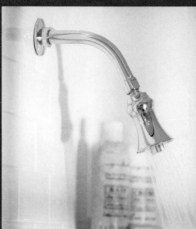

far left New chrome tub fixtures coordinate with fixtures elsewhere in the room. Single-handle faucets such as this one provide ease of operation.

left The fluted showerhead complements the other bath accessories and fixtures. A small built-in corner shelf provides just enough space for shower necessities.

Radiant Radiator

Old radiators can certainly remain functional long after they've lost their luster. When the homeowners were remodeling this bathroom, they treated the radiator to a new coat of paint in keeping with the sleek style of the '30s period room. They took the radiator to an automotive parts company where it was sandblasted and then given an electrostatic charge. The charge allowed powdered pigment to stick to the radiator as it passed through a high temperature oven. The extreme temperature melted the powdered pigment, which adhered to the metal, giving it a lustrous finish.

right Like the black tiles that run around the base of the wall and the black diamonds inserted in the floor, the black radiator becomes an accent in this primarily white bathroom. Making the radiator a point of focus rather than attempting to disguise it is a good example of combining form and function.

Deep in a country setting, this bath reflects nature's soft colors—muted greens, cedar, and maple. Natural light floods through the bay window—so much so that recessed lighting and sconces are rarely used during the day. The wall between the outdoors and indoors seems to disappear, especially when there's time for a relaxing soak with a view of the treetops. Grab bars to assist exit and entry to the platform tub would be a good addition to this bath.

Barn Beauty

The addition of a master bath creates a serene retreat in a barn that has been transformed into a home. The new space respects the architecture of the past.

American barns are fast disappearing. Sprawling suburbs and new farming practices are changing the landscape where these relics once symbolized the rural way of life. If not destroyed by age, the wood from barns is recycled and used in houses and offices for ambience. Barn timbers are prized because they are strong and straight and have a tight grain. Their weathered authenticity lends a sense of history to new houses.

Some homeowners, however, place great value on restoring barns to their original beauty. This master bath—an addition to a barn that was rescued and turned into a home— represents an effort to respect the lines of the building's original architecture while offering a restful retreat with modern-day comforts.

A respectful nod to barn architecture, the lines of the ceiling follow those of gambrel roofs, which were incorporated into late-19th-century barns to increase storage capacity for the haymow. Although purely decorative, cedar beams impart a rustic feel.

Natural Inspiration

The subdued palette in this bathroom is based on nature's colors. The ceiling sports cedar beams, and the cabinets are light maple. Gray-green ceramic tiles measuring 12×12 inches grace the platform and floor. The rough-textured matte finish is slip-resistant. For decorative flair, a minimal amount of stained glass echoes the lavender and green floral pattern on cream wallpaper.

Afternoon sunshine floods the bathroom through the bay window. Glass block filters light into the privacy compartment and shower stall on either side of the platform tub.

right A green-black countertop and backsplash complement the tone of the ceramic floor tiles. Polished brass fixtures match the style of those used in the tub and double shower. The creamy color of the sink coordinates with those of the bathtub and shower.

below The careful attention to detail in the ceiling gives a respectful nod to barn architecture with the line of the gambrel roof, constructed of cedar beams and tongue-and-groove wood strips. Wood reflects light warmly, providing a rich and textured atmosphere throughout the room.

Soaring Yet Private

Creating private areas in large spaces allows several members of the family to be in the bathroom at the same time. Zoning spaces for multiple users is an efficient and effective means of getting busy families out the door in the morning. The height of the ceiling in the chamber that houses the toilet and bidet could make the room seem dark and gloomy. The problem was solved by installing glass blocks at the top of the wall to cast natural light into the space and create dramatic contrasts of light and shadow on the ceiling and beams.

below A towel holder and matching soap dish are installed within easy reach of the bidet. While the scale of the areas in this bathroom is large, smart placement of accessories keeps the verticality from being overwhelming.

above Located in a privacy compartment to the left of the tub, the toilet and bidet have traditional shapes and fixtures. The exposed ceiling and beams emphasize the lines of the gambrel roof.

Good Textures

Strong Use of Stone and Tile

With wood being a dominant feature, the subdued color palette appropriately draws from nature.

- Gray-green ceramic tiles (**above**) grace the tub platform and the floor. The rough-textured matte finish is slip-resistant to ensure safe footing. To break the expanse of gray-green tiles, a border of earth-tone diamonds, dark rectangles, and squares was installed.
- Two inlaid tile borders (**above right**) add detail and break up the height of the shower stall.
- Green-black granite with rounded edges (**right**) is used for countertops and the stepped shelves that surround and define the boundaries of the vanity.
- The tile border (**below right**) continues around the perimeter of the main space.

smooth **TRANSITIONS**

Select flooring and countertops that will resist stain and wear and be easy to maintain. Regardless of choice, be aware that tile may raise the level of the finished floor above that in an adjacent room. It's essential to check the underlayment when figuring the height of the new floor. Different heights between rooms may require transitions to flow smoothly.

Glass Block

Patterned glass block, used effectively in this bathroom, lets in natural light without glare and preserves privacy.

Glass block is a good sound and heat insulator and comes in squares, hexagons, and corner units. Blocks are available in different colors and are 6, 8, and 12 inches square. For exterior walls and permanent solid glass block windows in the shower, the most common thickness is 3⅞ inches. Block surfaces are available in various patterns, from rippled to clear. Some have inserts that improve privacy and reduce heat loss.

Preassembled units custom-made to fit any opening are available, but they are heavy, are hard to manage, and probably will require professional installation.

For the look of glass without the expense and the weight, consider acrylic block windows. They come assembled in a frame to fit the opening and are comparable in price to many regular glass windows. Glass block windows don't open, but some come with built-in ventilation. If this is not the case, external ventilation will be required to remove moisture and odors.

above Although colors are subtle, texture is a powerful design element, particularly where it meets in this corner. Sunlight on the glass block appears to ripple and bounce, emphasizing the uneven surface. The intricate pattern of curving leaves and flowers is a calming counterpoint to the lines.

left To be effective, glass block walls require a strong natural light source. The large bay window over the platform tub casts strong light into the room, allowing the block to transmit light into adjoining areas.

light SHOW

Some homeowners use artificial light and glass block to heighten decorative effect. For example, a track with fiber-optic lighting can be fitted within a block wall. Attached to a control, the light—its intensity and mood—can be adjusted with a switch.

Shower Power

above A built-in bench in the shower holds bathing accessories and creates an opportunity to sit and relax under a comforting stream of water at the beginning or end of the day.

left Natural light filters through glass block and bounces off pale tile walls in this roomy double shower. Fixtures are spare and straightforward. A soap dish and a corner shelf are within easy reach. Many soap dishes and other similar accessories are designed to be installed directly on top of ceramic tiles.

Details

below Wide six-panel dressing room doors and vanities mirror each other. Partial walls contribute to the open look. On one side of the double doors that open to the bedroom is a linen closet; on the other side, bifold doors lead to an elevator that can be used in the future should a family member have difficulty going up and down stairs.

above Maple bifold doors reveal a linen closet.

above One of the large walk-in dressing rooms offers convenience for the homeowner.

above The custom-built mirror frame and medicine cabinet are made of maple, as is the cabinetry.

Bathed in light from three double-hung windows and an arched window, the tub is the room's focal point. While designed for the lady of the house—who prefers a daily soak rather than a quick shower—it accommodates two.

Serene Classic

This soothing retreat highlights traditional lines, creamy woodwork, and pale marble on the floors and countertops.

A couple with seven children—four at home—created this 10×30-foot getaway where they can prepare peacefully for the hectic day or relax in the evening. Working with an architect, they took an evenhanded approach. The classical style exhibits harmonious lines, while the husband's and wife's spaces function according to their individual needs.

Opposite the tub, dual vanities flank the room's entrance. Both feature round ceramic sinks, polished brass fittings, and generous counter space. Large mirrors framed to match the room's woodwork are paired with frosted-glass sconces. On her side of the room, a portion of the vanity is lowered to desk level to use to apply makeup and style hair. A small scrollwork chair adds detail to the look of the bathroom.

Allowing two people to share space comfortably is the obvious advantage to a large bathroom like this one. The openness also discourages steamy mirrors and humidity and proves that style and substance can be combined in one gracious setting.

His and Hers

An area that allows a couple to share space, then claim zones of privacy is ideal. The husband, for instance, prefers to shower quickly in the morning, while his wife likes to unwind in the evening by taking a soothing bath. Fortunately, they can both indulge. The shower and the tub areas have something in common: polished brass fixtures that run hot and cold water—no bells, no whistles.

above Polished brass faucets and fixtures provide subtle shine and an old-fashioned touch. The fixtures will keep their gleam if gently cared for over the years. Do not apply ammonia, bleach, or other chemicals to polished brass. Instead clean with mild soap and water, then blot the moisture with a soft cloth.

left The oval freestanding tub, its shape reminiscent of an old-fashioned claw-foot tub, has a ceramic tile base and polished brass grab rail.

top A privacy compartment adjacent to the man's vanity houses both a toilet and a bidet.

left The shower stall, positioned behind the man's vanity, is wrapped in marble, though small skid-resistant floor tiles ensure safety. The ribbed-glass door adds texture. A vapor-proof fixture recessed in the ceiling supplements natural light.

Elegant Marble

Like all the woodwork, the moldings are painted a deep cream. The base molding has three basic components: the cap, the baseboard, and the shoe, where it meets the marble floor. Laid in 12×12-inch squares, this natural stone is the color of oatmeal, with finely striéd tan, yellow, cream, and light brown tones. Though cool to the touch, the surface warms the room.

The same marble squares also cover the countertops of the dual vanities. The varying tones in the stone add texture to this surface, which is durable yet refined. However, marble can absorb stains and dirt. Sealing makes it less porous, but does not eliminate risk of marring. The details that make marble so attractive also put it at risk. Veining gives the illusion of texture, but it weakens the stone. Marble also is difficult to repair.

Tasteful Restraint

Classical style is uncluttered. Generally, materials are few in number and used consistently. For example, the surface-mounted sinks repeat the chamois color of the tub, and marble is used on the floor and countertops and in the shower. The sink, tub, and shower fixtures are polished brass.

Balance is also a hallmark of this style. Above the tub, the arched window and three double-hung windows form a symmetrical arrangement.

right A lowered section of the vanity allows the lady of the house to sit while applying makeup and doing hair. The wrought-iron white chair before the makeup vanity displays Victorian flourishes in its fan back. The tufted cushion adds a touch of pattern and texture.

below Steps from the oversize soaking tub, the woman's vanity area is refined while providing storage. As in the man's vanity area, a pair of classical frosted-glass sconces flank each mirror. Simple glass knobs embellish every door and drawer.

A straight-line axis continues from the tub to the master bedroom, with elements paired on either side: vanities, mirrors, and the double doors leading into the hallway, which has closets in each wall. On either side of the tub is a pairing of doors: the linen closet behind the wife's vanity and a dual shower behind the husband's.

below The marble gives way to oak flooring in the hallway that leads into the master bedroom, which also has cool green walls.

left A roomy closet behind the woman's vanity provides shelf space for towels, bed linens, extra grooming supplies, and other items. Sufficient clearance space allows the closet doors to swing open without disturbing anyone using the vanity.

right The bidet is located away from the rest of the bathroom area to ensure privacy.

Attention to detail—evident in the walls, window treatment, mirror, fixtures, and art—gives this powder room an elegant feel.

Small and Stunning

Small bathrooms such as this dramatic powder room present an opportunity to create a stunning look.

This powder room is only 5½×6 feet yet makes a dramatic statement with rich, warm walls and simple yet elegant fixtures. The room, located off a hallway between the garage and the kitchen, is convenient for guests, yet offers privacy because it is not directly adjacent to an entertainment area.

Faux Finishes

A powder room provides the perfect canvas for dramatic faux finishes that might be overwhelming in larger rooms. The walls in this bath were treated to a skip trowel application of plaster to plaster wall board that produces unique patterns and texture on the walls. Next the walls were painted with a matte orange paint, then sponge painted with black paint mixed with faux finish glaze. Colorless glaze is used to provide transparency and time to work with the faux effect. The result is a rich wall color with depth.

Because of the layers of color used in a faux treatment, it's difficult to know how the finished wall will look until all steps are complete. The homeowners were concerned that the orange walls were too bright until the black glaze was applied. Now they love the final look. Before applying a faux treatment to walls, try the entire technique on a piece of scrap plywood to make sure you like the finished look and to perfect your technique.

below The warm tones in the light sconces and mirror frame coordinate with the rich, warm color of the walls in this powder room.

above To create the rich wall treatment, the contractor applied plaster to the walls with varied hand movements so that each wall has a unique pattern and texture. Next walls were painted with a matte orange paint, then sponge painted with black paint mixed with faux finish glaze.

below Typically, small tiles are used in small rooms. Here the homeowner selected large 18×18-inch floor tiles for a small powder room. The large tiles serve to visually enlarge the space and provide a strong anchor for the dramatic walls.

Selecting Color

Small rooms can handle intense, deep color as is evidenced by this powder room. When selecting color for a powder room, bring home several paint samples and look at the color in the room. Check the color at several times during the day and evening, because natural light affects the perception of color. Think about when the room will be used most often and look at the color in those conditions. A powder room such as this one receives most use at night when guests are visiting, so be sure to check the color after dark with the lighting that will be used in the room.

top right and right Brushed nickel fixtures complement the warm palette used in this bathroom. The brushed nickel towel bar echoes the finish and shape of the faucet. The simple lines of these fixtures work well against the strong backdrop created by the faux wall treatment.

below left This window treatment features a curved bar that brings the fabric slightly into the room, adding depth to the walls.

below right The slim portrait toilet fits easily into this powder room. Framed prints complement the wall color and provide a finished look to the room.

Bath time can be a treat instead of a struggle with fun yet simple bath accessories. A bright rubber duck tub spout cushion protects young bathers and continues the colorful child-friendly decorating scheme of this bathroom.

Splish-Splash in the Bath

A standard bathroom can quickly and easily be transformed into a children's bath with a few accessories you can update as your child grows.

Creating a bathroom that grows with your child can be simple and affordable. Toddlers don't need a pint-size vanity and toilet to be comfortable and safe in the bathroom; and teens can live without cartoon-inspired ceramic tiles. This family bathroom with tub/shower combination, standard vanity with sink, and toilet compartment is typical of many American homes. The basic decor is simple and easy to change. Colorful, child-friendly accessories plus easy-to-install safety features allow the room to serve the needs of a toddler. Swap out the accessories for those that appeal to a more sophisticated taste and the room will be ready for a teen. And when the family reaches empty-nest stage, the bath can serve overnight guests with a simple update.

right A few colorful accessories and a border with a children's theme are all it takes to create a bathroom that makes bath time fun for little ones. As the children grow, accessories can easily be swapped, allowing the bath to grow with the children.

Combining Safety with Fun

This bath is ready for a toddler. Whimsical accessories, such as the duck shower curtain and baby animal wallpaper border, are inexpensive touches that define the room, yet can easily be replaced in a few years when the child outgrows them. The tile floors are durable for children of any age, and are easy to clean.

above Lower drawers filled with bath toys allow small children to get out and put away their own things, and keep bath-time fun close to the tub.

left Plastic tumblers, toothbrush holders, and other accessories are a wise choice for children's bathrooms.

Be Safe

A step stool with rubber feet that prevent sliding allows a toddler to use a standard height vanity with minimal assistance. Hidden safety features such as child-resistant cabinet latches and toilet-lid locks help child proof the room. Keep all medicines and vitamins locked out of children's reach even when using child-resistant latches. Anti-scald devices help to prevent burns from hot water. Lowering the temperature on water heaters to 120 degrees also minimizes the risk of burns.

above A variety of child-resistant devices, such as cabinet latches and toilet-lid locks, are available to prevent children from opening doors, drawers, and toilets. Even with safety latches installed, keep breakables out of children's reach and lock away vitamins and medicines.

left Avoid sharp edges by selecting a vanity with curved corners to help prevent bruises and cuts.

far left Step stools allow young children to reach the sink. Rubber feet prevent the stool from sliding on wet tile.

left GFCI (ground fault circuit interrupter) receptacles are required by code in areas where water is present. GFCIs sense any shock hazard and shut off a circuit or receptacle. Even with a GFCI, appliances should be kept away from water and unplugged when not in use.

Adapting for Older Children

Simply swapping the shower curtain and wallpaper border with a more sophisticated design, selected with the input of an older child, will update this bath. New accents and accessories will blend well with the basic plaid fabrics used in the window treatment. The footstool can be repositioned under the window near the tub to hold bath towels and a robe.

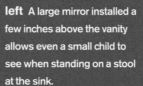

left A large mirror installed a few inches above the vanity allows even a small child to see when standing on a stool at the sink.

above Tile can withstand the splashing that is part of a child's bath time fun, but can be cold for little feet. Use washable bath mats and rugs with non-slip backing for safety.

above A dressed-up roller shade provides privacy and coordinates with the lighthearted decorating scheme of the bathroom. Roller shades are a safe window treatment for children's spaces because they operate without cords.

above Install a hand-held sprayer in the tub for children who are too young for a shower, but are old enough to rinse themselves off after a sudsy bath.

Touch-Up for Tweens and Teens

Another change of the shower curtain and wallpaper border—and this time the window treatment as well—can satisfy the changing tastes of a preteen or teenager. Ample storage provided by the vanity cabinets in this bathroom ensure that a teen has plenty of room for grooming supplies. If neutral walls are too bland to suit your teen, you can feel comfortable handing over the paintbrush; it will be simple to repaint the walls when tastes change again.

above A small linen closet separates the tub and toilet, providing some privacy to both areas without sacrificing the space needed to enclose the toilet in a separate room.

above The National Kitchen and Bath Association recommends having a compartment at least 36 inches wide and 66 inches long for a separate toilet room. When space is more limited, as in this bath, create the illusion of a separate room without adding the door.

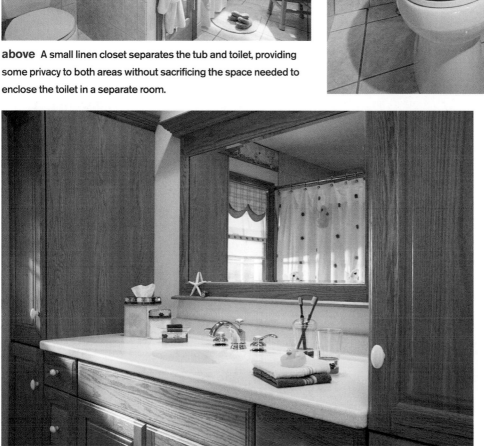

left Generous counter space puts children's bathroom necessities such as toothbrushes and plastic tumblers within easy reach. Tall cabinets on both sides of the vanity allow each family member to have separate storage space.

Planning

Making a workable and thorough plan to realize your new bathroom is probably the most important phase of a remodeling project. Without careful planning, the best design will fall short of expectations.

Now that you've gone through Chapters 1 and 2, you're ready to start planning your new bathroom. The most important advice is **do your homework** and **take your time**! Rushing decisions will only lead to frustration. You could well end up with something that is beautiful but not practical. With careful planning and attention to detail, you can create a bathroom that will provide years of pleasure.

CHAPTER 3 CONTENTS

left Putting in a new bathroom isn't easy; in fact, you need all the help you can get. Home centers provide a great support system for homeowners who are interested in a new bathroom. They offer design services, products, and even installation. Consulting professionals as you plan a new bath will save you time and money, not to mention a few headaches along the way.

Getting Started

Planning your bath (and staying on budget) may seem a daunting task, but if you take a deep breath and work through the process one step at a time, you will achieve your goals.

Some Very Important Information

Many people have unpleasant experiences installing a new bathroom because they don't plan carefully and they don't give themselves enough time to complete the project. If you want a new bathroom in time for Christmas, don't start demolition the day after Thanksgiving. Construction is a business of surprises. No matter how thorough you are and how skilled and dedicated your contractor is, things will go wrong. Shipments could be delayed, parts could be damaged on delivery, there may be problems behind the walls, and the weather may not cooperate. The more room you have to compensate for the unexpected, the more successful and satisfying your experience will be.

Read This Chapter

Get an overview of the planning process by reading this chapter (breeze through Chapter 4 as well) before you begin to actually put things on paper. A bit of general knowledge will help you sort out and then make sense of what may at first seem to be a complicated and overwhelming process.

Get Specific

Start by charting your family's daily routine. Evaluate the features of your current bath, reflecting on what works well and what you hope to improve. Talk with other family members who will use the new bath. In your current arrangement, do people trip over one another trying to use the bath at the same time each day? As the next step, consider how you see your bath being used: relaxation, reading, working, and dressing; or maybe you prefer a no-frills utilitarian space. Are more windows, light, and a view a major priority?

Keep a Journal

For a week or so keep a journal to record how your bath is used and describe any aggravations caused by the existing layout. Note times the bath is "too busy." List inconveniences in terms of storage and layout. Jot down times you'd love to relax in your whirlpool tub, if only you had one. Or make a note if you do have a whirlpool or other large tub, but there's never enough hot water to fill it. Do any family members have privacy issues, either within the bath or from too much open exposure to the outside world?

Fill Out the Checklists

The comprehensive checklists that follow in this chapter are meant to be useful tools throughout your planning process. You may find it helpful to make detailed notes about the elements in your current bath while developing your plan for the bath of your dreams. Prioritizing the features that are most important to you will be useful when the inevitable budget trade-offs become necessary. And don't forget to look to the future. A well-designed bath suits not only your current needs and circumstances but also accommodates lifestyle changes in the future.

No Mystery

This chapter takes the mystery out of two of the most critical parts of the planning process: developing a budget and sketching a detailed floor plan.

How It All Fits

Basic information on specifications and clearances for fixtures and products is included so that you can have some idea of how the elements of your bath will all fit together as you devise a plan.

Make a Floor Plan

When you understand your needs and the basics of products and materials, you're ready to create a floor plan and start making some decisions about budget.

Develop a Budget

Getting the most bathroom for your money is only logical. Making a budget and sticking to it will relieve the inevitable stress that comes from preparing to spend a big chunk of your hard-earned money. Budgets not only set basic parameters, they help you track expenses and the progress of the job. The hardest part of any budget, of course, is sticking to it.

Great Advice

Equally important, you'll find great advice on determining the types of professionals you should hire; selecting professionals to interview; conducting interviews; hiring the building or design professional who is right for your job; entering into a contract for the project; and working with the professionals throughout the entire process.

---

sweet INSPIRATION

Whether you want to give your bath a simple face-lift or build an entirely new addition, do not rush into making decisions. At this stage, allow yourself to dream and gather ideas.

- Collect magazine pictures that depict room styles and elements that appeal to you.
- Talk with friends about their remodeling experiences and visit developer's open houses for ideas.
- Surf the Internet for design ideas and product information.
- Collect product brochures and catalogs (you can order them from manufacturers or find them at home centers; you also will find lists of manufacturers in the resource sections of many books and magazines).
- Buy home repair books or check them out from the library. Learn the basics (including key terminology) about plumbing, wiring, venting, and construction so that you'll be prepared when it's time to consult professionals.
- Keep a small notebook in your purse or coat pocket. You'll be ready to jot down notes in case you have a great idea or spot an appealing product.

Resources pile up fast, so you'll need to devise a record-keeping system. Use a thick zippered ring binder with dividers and pockets. To get started, turn to page 7 and adapt the table of contents as a way to organize your binder. For example, you might have two major sections labeled Style and Function. In the Style section, you could label dividers for color schemes, decorating themes, and specific elements, such as sinks, tubs, showers, surface materials, and accessories, that contribute to the look of your bath.

Use the Function section to track practical information about activity centers and layouts. Use this chapter for general information about cabinet and counter space guidelines, appliances, ventilation, lighting, and electrical and plumbing requirements.

Make sure each divider has plenty of paper for the notes you'll take. At this stage, allow yourself to record your wildest notions. Include clear acetate sheets so that you can readily store—and see—articles, pictures, brochures, and other clippings. If you gather a lot of material, surface, color, and fabric samples, store them in clear plastic boxes with labels.

Lifestyle Checklists

If you want to remodel an existing bath, you may be tempted to jump right in and select new fixtures, sinks, tubs, showers, and surface materials. But experts agree that the best approach is to first think through the positive aspects and the drawbacks of your current bath, then use that evaluation to identify the key features that will be the most important to you in your dream bath. Use the checklists in this chapter to:

■ Label the type of bath.

■ Identify the users of the current bath.

■ Determine how well the current bath functions.

■ Identify features that could be changed to better suit particular needs.

When assessing your current bathroom, take into account how you and your family use it daily, how often you have guests, and how you anticipate using the bath in the years to come.

If your bath project is a new addition, much of the same thought process applies. Weigh the positive and negative features of other baths in your home. These checklists are designed to prompt note taking and to stimulate questions. You will reference and add to this information throughout the planning stage. You can photocopy this checklist and others to store in your journal. They will come in handy when you map your new bath and talk with professionals. For general information on pricing see page 117.

USERS OF THE BATH	YES	NO
Does/will one adult use the bath?	☐	☐
Does/will two adults use the bath?	☐	☐
Does/will one child use the bath?	☐	☐
Does an adult bathe a child in the bathtub?	☐	☐
Does/will more than one child use the bath?	☐	☐
Does/will one teenager use the bath?	☐	☐
Does/will more than one teenager use the bath?	☐	☐
Does/will a person with disabilities use the bath?	☐	☐
Does/will an older adult use the bath?	☐	☐
Do/will guests frequently use this bath?	☐	☐
Is there adequate room in the current bath for the number of people using it?	☐	☐

ACCESS AND PRIVACY	YES	NO
Does/will the bath serve one bedroom?	☐	☐
Does/will the bath serve several bedrooms?	☐	☐
Do you desire:		
More doorways in and out of the bath?	☐	☐
Fewer doorways in and out of the bath?	☐	☐
Do you want to relocate a doorway away from a public area?	☐	☐
Do the windows compromise privacy?	☐	☐
If so, do you want to replace it with glass or other material that obscures the view?	☐	☐
If so, do you want to relocate it?	☐	☐
Do you desire:		
More room around the sink(s) and vanity area(s)?	☐	☐
More room around the toilet?	☐	☐
A privacy compartment with a door for the toilet?	☐	☐
A semiprivate compartment for the toilet?	☐	☐
More clearance in front of the tub or shower?	☐	☐
Does your bath require improved soundproofing because of:		
Uninsulated pipes?	☐	☐
Pipes made of inadequate materials?	☐	☐
Inadequate wall insulation?	☐	☐
Inadequate floor insulation?	☐	☐
Does your bath have adequate ventilation:		
A fan?	☐	☐
Window(s)?	☐	☐

UNIVERSAL DESIGN	YES	NO
Are the doorways wide enough for a wheelchair?	☐	☐
Does the door swing into the bathroom?	☐	☐
Or, does the door swing out of the bathroom?	☐	☐
Would you prefer a pocket door?	☐	☐
Is there at least 5 square feet of turnaround space?	☐	☐
Do you need an elevator?	☐	☐
Would a walk-in closet be helpful?	☐	☐
If so, does it need lower shelving/hanging units?	☐	☐
Would it be used by more than one person?	☐	☐
Is the storage area accessible to a wheelchair user?	☐	☐
Do you need wheelchair access for:	☐	☐
Room under the sink(s) and vanity area(s)?	☐	☐
Room beside the toilet?	☐	☐
Clearance in front of the tub or shower?	☐	☐
Is your shower/tub adequate in size for the user?	☐	☐
Do you need a roll-in shower stall?	☐	☐

Bathroom Layout Checklists

Study the various bath categories and determine which one best describes the type of bath you want. (See pages 20–23.) Then check off the following lists. For general information on pricing see page 117.

MASTER BATH

One long vanity with mirror and two sinks	☐
Dual vanities, each with a sink and mirror	☐
Vanities for users of different heights	☐
Toilet compartment	☐
Semi-enclosed toilet space	☐
Bidet	☐
Separate tub and shower	☐
Double shower	☐
Oversize tub	☐
Whirlpool	☐
Sauna	☐
Steam shower	☐
Showerheads at different heights	☐
Two separate baths	☐
A separate powder room or dressing room in the master suite	☐
Two walk-in dressing rooms	☐
Stacked washer and dryer unit	☐
Fireplace	☐
Media area	☐
Coffee maker	☐
Speakers in the ceiling	☐
Shower sound systems	☐
Mini workstation: small table, chair, and phone	☐

FAMILY OR GENERAL-PURPOSE BATH

Sink	☐
Bathtub	☐
Shower	☐
Tub/shower combination	☐
One long vanity with mirror and two sinks	☐
Separate vanity/grooming area	☐
Toilet compartment	☐
Semi-enclosed toilet space	☐
Storage for linens	☐
Storage for each user	☐
Laundry center	☐
Stacked washer and dryer unit	☐

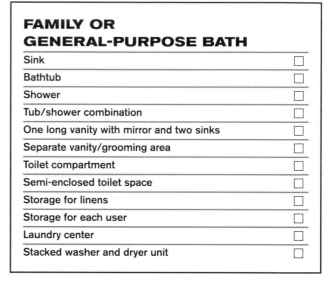

CHILDREN'S BATH

Nonslip surfaces (ceramic tile with matte finish or smaller tiles)	☐
Pressure-balanced faucets	☐
Durable countertop and vanity (laminate, for example)	☐
Two separate vanity areas and shared tub/shower and toilet areas	☐
Counters at standard heights with built-in step stool	☐
Lower set of towel bars	☐
Tub/shower combination	☐
Access between children's bedrooms	☐
Easy-care wall surface (gloss paint finish or scrubbable, removable wallpaper)	☐
Simple colors and patterns that do not seem too trendy or childish	☐
Inexpensive, changeable accessories	☐

GUEST BATH

Sink and toilet (added on into space of laundry room, closet, or mudroom)	☐
Sink, toilet, tub/shower combination	☐
Dual sinks, toilet, tub/shower combination	☐
Sink and toilet separated by pocket door from tub/shower	☐
Sink and toilet separated by pocket door from tub/shower with private access to guest room	☐

Bath Features and Products Checklists

Evaluate the features, fixtures, and other elements in your current bath to help you decide what to keep or change.

Information about many of these choices are in Chapter 4. For general information on pricing see page 117.

SINKS AND FIXTURES	YES	NO
Does your current sink please you?	☐	☐
Size (adequate for washing delicate garments, for example)?	☐	☐
Height?	☐	☐
Shape?	☐	☐
Color?	☐	☐
Material?	☐	☐
Do your current fixtures please you?	☐	☐
Number and type of faucet handles?	☐	☐
Faucet height?	☐	☐
Style?	☐	☐
Finish?	☐	☐
Functionality (ease of turning on and off)?	☐	☐
Temperature control?	☐	☐

COUNTERTOPS AND BACKSPLASHES	YES	NO
Does your current countertop please you?	☐	☐
Convenient location?	☐	☐
Enough space around the sink?	☐	☐
Enough space for everyday grooming (room for toiletries, brushes, etc.)?	☐	☐
Height (multiple heights for different users)?	☐	☐
Shape?	☐	☐
Color?	☐	☐
Material?	☐	☐
Does your current backsplash please you?	☐	☐
Color?	☐	☐
Material?	☐	☐
Ease of cleaning?	☐	☐

STORAGE

	YES	NO
Is current storage convenient and adequate for:		
Toiletries?	☐	☐
Makeup?	☐	☐
Lotion?	☐	☐
Shampoo?	☐	☐
Shaving supplies?	☐	☐
Is current storage convenient and adequate for:		
Bath towels and washcloths?	☐	☐
Guest towels?	☐	☐
Bed linens?	☐	☐
Blankets?	☐	☐
Throws?	☐	☐
Pillows?	☐	☐
Beach towels?	☐	☐
Other linens?	☐	☐
Is current storage convenient and adequate for:		
Toilet tissue?	☐	☐
Bath and hand soap?	☐	☐
Cleaning supplies?	☐	☐
Do you desire additional storage?	☐	☐
Do you desire a different storage configuration?	☐	☐
Are you satisfied with the features of your current vanities, cabinets, and shelving?		
Convenient location?	☐	☐
Style?	☐	☐
Height?	☐	☐
Shape?	☐	☐
Color?	☐	☐
Material?	☐	☐

into the
FUTURE

As part of this analysis, think about how long you plan to stay in your home. You may not know for sure. However, consider whether you plan to move when your children leave home. If not, will your children's bath be used in the future by guests? Are you planning functionality with both potential uses in mind? Thinking through these types of issues ensures that your bath will serve you well in the coming years.

STORAGE *(continued)*

	YES	NO
Do you have or are you planning for:		
Conventional double vanity?	☐	☐
Individual vanities?	☐	☐
Furniture-style vanity?	☐	☐
Multiple-height countertops?	☐	☐
Built-in makeup area with lower countertop?	☐	☐
Two pedestal sinks?	☐	☐
Glass doors for some of your cabinetry?	☐	☐
Do you have/want additional storage options, such as:		
Medicine cabinets?	☐	☐
Drawers?	☐	☐
Above-counter drawers?	☐	☐
Linen closet?	☐	☐
Open shelving?	☐	☐
Open shelving below counter height for children?	☐	☐
Tall-narrow cabinet near toilet for scrub brushes and cleaners?	☐	☐
Built-in niche in closet for laundry baskets?	☐	☐
Storage for kids' needs (toys, books, and bath supplies)?	☐	☐
Fold-down shelf door that serves as a step stool for children?	☐	☐
Built-in window seat with pullout drawers?	☐	☐
Rolling/mobile shelves or storage unit?	☐	☐
Towel bars, hooks, and racks?	☐	☐
Heated towel racks or bars?	☐	☐
Towel warming drawer?	☐	☐
Hand towel rings?	☐	☐
Grab bars?	☐	☐
Walls reinforced for current or future grab bars?	☐	☐
Freestanding furniture?	☐	☐
Adjacent closet for bathroom storage?	☐	☐

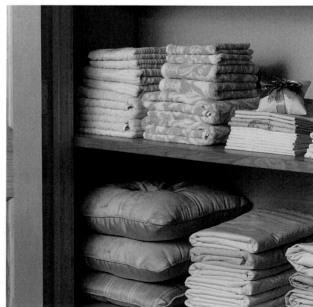

SHOWER/TUB COMBINATIONS

	YES	NO
Does your current shower/tub please you?	☐	☐
Size?	☐	☐
Height?	☐	☐
Shape?	☐	☐
Color?	☐	☐
Material?	☐	☐
Are you satisfied with the following features of your current fixture(s):		
Number and type of handles?	☐	☐
Faucet style?	☐	☐
Finish?	☐	☐
Functionality (ease of turning on and off)?	☐	☐
Temperature control?	☐	☐

SHOWERS

	YES	NO
Does your current shower please you?	☐	☐
Size?	☐	☐
Height?	☐	☐
Shape?	☐	☐
Color?	☐	☐
Material?	☐	☐
If you desire a separate shower or shower/tub combination, are you considering:		
Shower door, curtain, or open shower?	☐	☐
If open, what features make it "splash-proof"?		
Curved tile door?	☐	☐
Ceiling showerhead so that water sprays straight down?	☐	☐
If door, what type?		
Framed clear glass?	☐	☐
Etched-glass door?	☐	☐
Frosted-glass panels?	☐	☐
Glass walls?	☐	☐

SHOWERHEADS

	YES	NO
Are you considering any of the following fixtures or features?		
Multiple showerheads?	☐	☐
Adjustable?	☐	☐
Wall-mount?	☐	☐
Top-mount?	☐	☐
Ceiling-mount "rain" showerhead?	☐	☐
Handheld?	☐	☐
Sliding bar?	☐	☐
Body spray and body mist?	☐	☐
Vertical shower spa?	☐	☐
Body spa shower panels?	☐	☐
Water-saving function?	☐	☐
Antiscald protection?	☐	☐

TUBS

	YES	NO
Do you like your current tub?	☐	☐
Are you considering the following styles?	☐	☐
Recessed?	☐	☐
Corner?	☐	☐
Freestanding?	☐	☐
Claw-foot?	☐	☐
Platform?	☐	☐
Tub with ledge/room to sit at one end?	☐	☐

TUB FIXTURES

	YES	NO
Do your current fixtures and features please you?	☐	☐
Number and type of handles?	☐	☐
Handheld sprayer?	☐	☐
Faucet height?	☐	☐
Style?	☐	☐
Finish?	☐	☐
Functionality (ease of turning on and off)?	☐	☐
Temperature control?	☐	☐

SPECIAL FIXTURES

	YES	NO
Do you desire any of the following:	☐	☐
Sauna?	☐	☐
Freestanding shower?	☐	☐
Built-in seating?	☐	☐
Steam shower?	☐	☐
Whirlpool?	☐	☐
Mini tub?	☐	☐
Soaking tub?	☐	☐
Japanese soaking tub?	☐	☐
Foot whirlpool?	☐	☐
Spa?	☐	☐
Waterfall faucet?	☐	☐
In-line or passive heater to help maintain water temperature?	☐	☐

TOILETS	YES	NO
Which type do you have/desire?		
One-piece?	☐	☐
Two-piece (elongated and rounded front)?	☐	☐
Toilet outfitted with seat warmer?	☐	☐
Kid-size toilet?	☐	☐
Toilet/bidet combination?	☐	☐
Size?	☐	☐
Height?	☐	☐
Shape?	☐	☐
Color?	☐	☐
Material?	☐	☐
Do your current fixtures please you?		
Style?	☐	☐
Finish?	☐	☐

BIDETS	YES	NO
Which type do you have/desire?		
Vertical spray in bowl center?	☐	☐
Integral filler?	☐	☐
Special spout (horizontal stream)?	☐	☐
Size?	☐	☐
Shape?	☐	☐
Color?	☐	☐
Material?	☐	☐
Do your current fixtures please you?		
Style?	☐	☐
Finish?	☐	☐

LIGHTING	YES	NO
Does your bath have adequate:		
Overhead lighting?	☐	☐
Vanity lighting (side fixtures)?	☐	☐
Do your windows and skylights equal 10 percent of the room's square footage?	☐	☐

FLOORING	YES	NO
Does your bath's current flooring please you?	☐	☐
If no, which material will you use in your new bath?	☐	☐
Vinyl?	☐	☐
Hardwood?	☐	☐
Laminate?	☐	☐
Carpet?	☐	☐
Ceramic tile?	☐	☐
Stone?	☐	☐

HIDDEN details

What about electrical codes, plumbing, heating and cooling, and ventilation? Some important planning pointers are provided below. And don't forget the detailed information about these systems later in this chapter.

- When selecting materials for your new bath, remember that the steamy, wet environment can be a breeding ground for mold and mildew. In your current bath, have any surfaces been damaged by leaks or excessive moisture? Is your wallpaper peeling or your floor warping? Is the tile uneven? The answers to these questions should help you evaluate the many materials choices available.
- Is your bath currently outfitted with a new, low-flow toilet?
- Are the pipes and walls in your bath well-insulated?
- Are your current fixtures difficult to clean as a result of design or placement?
- Do you have sufficient heating in your current bath?
- Does the exhaust fan satisfactorily move out the steamy air after a shower?
- Plumbing reminder: Significant plumbing considerations (and costs) will arise if you move the location of your sink and/or install additional sinks in new locations.
- Electrical circuits: Evaluate the number of electrical circuits you will need. The right time to add extra electrical outlets and wiring is when the walls are down. Make sure you have enough outlets in the bath. Don't forget about a hair dryer, curling iron, vacuum cleaner, TV, clock, music system or radio, and coffeepot.

left A soft but rich color palette and candlelight make this master bathroom a romantic getaway or a comforting place to meditate on the events of the day. The detailed edge of the solid-surfacing countertop on the vanity echoes the paneled molding on the platform that frames the whirlpool bathtub.

General Guidelines

It is helpful to review guidelines for minimum clearance recommendations and fixture placement, which are recommended by the National Kitchen and Bath Association (NKBA) and other experts. Use this information to analyze the available space; then consider all of the recommended clearance guidelines and see whether your dream bath can be accomplished in the available space. If not, you have the knowledge to plan another layout or consider an expansion—if that is feasible given your space and budgetary constraints.

Remember that these are only guidelines. Some rules may not apply to your layout or particular needs. Your bath may work better if your available area allows you to include storage space and elbow room beyond that recommended by the guidelines. For more information on NKBA, see page 186.

tight squeeze?
WHAT TO DO

Many baths have to fit into fairly small spaces, which can lead to interesting design challenges. Here are possible solutions:

- Shower only or shower/tub combo instead of both.
- Place shower in a corner.
- For tubs, consider a nonstandard size or shape, corner tub, or other type specifically scaled for small spaces.
- Consider eliminating the tub and installing a roomy shower.
- Install one sink instead of two.
- Install a pedestal sink instead of a vanity (consider adding a narrow ledge/shelf to the wall behind the sink for storage).
- Use a toilet/bidet combo instead of separate units.
- "Steal" space from an adjoining bedroom, closet, or dead-end hallway, or bump out exterior walls.
- Eliminate clutter: Provide adequate storage space.
- Use special cabinetry features and fittings and creative shelving.
- Install recessed medicine cabinets.
- Buy vanity or cabinet drawers that have electrical outlets; use and store appliances in the same place.
- Consider pocket doors.
- Use design elements (color, shape, structure, pattern, texture, windows, skylights, artificial lighting, mirrors, glass, and shiny metal fixtures) to create a space that feels and functions "bigger" than its physical dimensions indicate.

Vanities, Countertops, and Mirrors

Vanities

Considering cabinet door size and drawer width is key to designing your vanity. Most experts agree that available space is better used with cabinet configurations calling for fewer doors and larger openings, as opposed to many doors and smaller openings.

For cabinets 24 inches or wider, two split doors are recommended over large single doors. Work to avoid extremely narrow doors and drawers—the storage space afforded by 9- and 12-inch widths is usually considered too small to be useful.

Dividing a space in half does not always provide the best storage results. For example, taking 60 inches of available space and dividing it in half would result in two 30-inch spaces, each of which would need two doors. But the same 60-inch area could be divided into areas that are different sizes—that is, one smaller area needing only one door and a second larger space with two doors.

Toiletries and towels are best stored near the tub; place this storage space 15 to 48 inches above the floor.

below The handiest storage is made up of fewer doors and larger openings. Larger openings allow bulky items such as towels and storage boxes to be easily removed.

top and above Well-planned storage makes your countertops available for decorative accents rather than cosmetic clutter. Put the most frequently used items, such as toothpaste and lotion, in the top drawer near the sink. Dividers or baskets in drawers aid organization of toiletries.

Countertops

- The height of a countertop should be designed to best accommodate the user(s). The standard height is 32 inches, but higher or lower may be more comfortable, depending on the height of the user.
- If your design calls for two vanities, consider making them different heights (perhaps one at 30–34 inches and the other at 34–42 inches). This would make them more comfortable for family members of different heights. Or design a section as a seated vanity.
- To eliminate sharp corners on countertops, use rounded or clipped corners and eased edges.

Note: solid-surfacing, quartz surface, and natural stone countertops require a template be made before they can be fabricated. You will probably need to use temporary tops for several weeks before the finished tops are installed!

right Standard cabinet units can be configured in many different combinations for custom looks. Study cabinet options and create a unique look for your bathroom.

Mirrors

- The bottom edge of a standard above-vanity mirror should be no more than 40 inches above the floor. (The height of the user determines your ultimate decision.)
- If the top of a mirror tilts away from the wall, the bottom edge can be 48 inches above the floor.

fairest
ONE OF ALL

- **To keep your mirror's good looks** for a long time, use only gentle cleansers. Clean, warm water is an option, as are glass cleaners, vinegar, and rubbing alcohol. But acid-, alkali-, and ammonia-base cleansers damage mirror edges and backing.
- **Spray cleaner onto a soft cloth,** then wipe. To remove tough spots, remoisten the cloth and rub. Avoid steel wool or abrasive cleaners, which scratch.
- **Keep your mirror as dry as possible.** Mount it above a backsplash or a few inches above the counter to prevent moisture buildup. If steam builds up on the mirror, run the bathroom fan to clear it.

Sinks

Sinks are available in a variety of shapes, with the most common shapes being rectangular, oval, round, and asymmetrical. Many materials are now available.

Vanity-Mounted Sinks

The most common vanity sinks are drop-in sinks, which are available as self-rimming or rimmed, undermount, vessel, flush-mounted, and integral, which might be made of solid-surfacing, stainless steel, stone, or composites.

Freestanding Sinks

There are two basic categories of freestanding sinks.
- Pedestal sinks are supported by a single base.
- Console sinks have either two or four legs and a "tabletop" surrounding the bowl, offering more countertop space.

Wall-Hung Sinks

- Wall-hung sinks are mounted to brackets that are attached to support members in the wall.

Sink Clearance

- In front of sinks, leave an open space of at least 30×48 inches (this can be either parallel or perpendicular).
- If the sink is wall-hung or another variety that provides knee space underneath, up to 19 of the recommended 48 inches may extend under the sink. Knee space, either open or adaptable, is recommended at every sink.
- On each side of the sink, leave at least 15 inches of clearance from the centerline of the sink to the closest fixture or sidewall.

Vanity with Two Sinks

- For sinks up to 30 inches wide, leave at least 30 inches of clearance between the sinks, measuring from the centerline of each sink.
- For larger sinks, plan for additional clearance to ensure plenty of elbow room when two people use the sinks simultaneously.

mounting
ACCESSORIES

- Towel bars are mounted approximately 52 inches from the finished floor. Towel bars over a toilet are mounted at a height to accommodate towel lengths.
- Towel bars or rings are mounted 16 to 18 inches above a countertop.
- Toilet paper holders are mounted approximately 26 inches above the finished floor.
- Soap dishes and toothbrush holders are mounted to be within easy reach of the sink.

Wall-mounted toilets have a tank "hidden" in the wall and discharge to the rear rather than through the floor. These toilets are quieter and offer a very contemporary look.

Basic Shapes

■ Standard toilets have round bowls and are 14 inches high. Models up to 17 inches high are available and are more comfortable for some users.

■ Toilets with elongated bowls are much more comfortable than standard toilets, but they are also more expensive.

Toilet Clearance

■ Leave 48×48 inches in front of toilets. (In tight spaces, you might be able to get away with 30×48 inches.)

■ On each side of a toilet, leave at least 16 inches (18 inches is preferred) of clear floor space from the centerline of the toilet to the closest fixture, sidewall, or other obstruction. (In tight spaces, you might be able to get away with 15 inches.)

■ If the toilet occupies a separate compartment or zone, the total area should measure at least 36 inches wide and 66 inches long.

■ If there is a door to the toilet compartment, remember to have an opening at least 32 inches wide.

■ For a swinging door, design the doors to swing out, and include adequate clearance space.

Toilets

While one-piece toilets provide a sleeker, more contemporary look and are easier to clean, two-piece toilets are the standard, traditional design. However, the distance between the floor drain and the wall (rough-in) will determine the style and availability of your new toilet. Common rough-in dimensions are 10, 12, and 14 inches with 12 inches being the most common.

easy-reach
TOILET PAPER

The best location for the toilet paper dispenser is usually about 8 inches in front of the edge of the toilet bowl and about 26 inches above the floor.

Bidets

Most homeowners who choose a bidet match it to the size and style of their toilet. Toilets and bidets are often sold together, and both are available in round and elongated styles.

Bidets are often more difficult to install than toilets, primarily because they are not as standardized. Also, bidets require a valve to turn the water on and off.

Bidet Clearance

■ The minimum floor space guidelines for a bidet are the same as those for toilets.

■ Toilets and bidets are often positioned next to each other. In this event, it's OK for the recommended open area for each to overlap; however, the centerline of the bidet should be at least 16 inches from that of the toilet.

Grab Bar Specifications

Grab Bars

- Grab bars are recommended for tubs, showers, and toilet areas.
- They should be 1¼ to 1½ inches in diameter, should extend 1½ inches from the wall, and should be designed to support a 300-pound load. Select grab bars with a slip-resistant surface.
- The recommended height for grab bars is 33 to 36 inches above the floor.
- Even if you do not plan to install grab bars immediately, it is smart to reinforce walls with dimensional lumber at the appropriate heights during construction so that you can add grab bars later.

Grab bars in the shower and tub area should be:
- At least 24 inches wide on the control wall.
- At least 12 inches wide on the head wall.
- At least 24 inches wide on the back wall, beginning no more than 12 inches from the control wall and no more than 15 inches from the head wall.
- If a second grab bar is installed on the back wall, it should be the same width as the grab bar above it and 9 inches above the bathtub deck.

Grab bars in shower stalls should be:
- Included on each surrounding wall (this is optional on a wall where there is a bench).
- No more than 9 inches shorter than the width of the wall to which they are attached.

Grab bars next to toilets should be:
- Located on the sidewall closest to the toilet.
- No more than 12 inches from the rear wall.
- At least 42 inches wide.
- If an optional secondary grab bar is included, it may be positioned on the rear wall no more than 6 inches from the sidewall, and it should be at least 24 inches wide.

Some suggested alternatives to grab bars in the toilet area include:
- Side bars attached below the toilet seat.
- A rail system that is mounted to the back wall and has perpendicular arms that flank the toilet seat.
- An electronic seat elevator.
- Rails suspended from the ceiling.

Tubs and Showers

Showers offer comfort, convenience, and, increasingly, luxury. Shower units separate from the tub are recommended whenever space will permit. This offers the opportunity for two people to bathe at the same time, and separate showers are generally considered to be safer than tub/shower combinations in terms of ease of getting in and out of the shower.

Prefabricated Shower Stalls

Most prefabricated shower surrounds are made of fiberglass that is finished with acrylic or a polyester gel coat. They can also be made of vinyl, plastic laminate, or synthetic stone. One-piece units are attractive and functional, but they are so large that they are best used in new construction. For remodeling projects, they can be very difficult to get into the bathroom. In most situations, you can opt for a multipiece surround kit, which can be assembled inside the bathroom. Prefabricated stalls are designed to fit against a wall or in a corner. With most of these units, either shower curtains or shower doors can be used, and these are typically purchased separately. Prefabricated units are considered easier to clean than custom stalls.

If you are interested in the latest high-tech showerheads, check with your builder before going with a prefab stall. Many of the prefabricated stalls cannot accommodate some of the elaborate valves and fittings.

Shower Pans

Prefabricated shower pans, or flooring pieces, are molded from plastic, terrazzo, or similar chipped stone. Instead of ordering a custom waterproof shower pan, you can combine a prefabricated type with prefabricated shower stalls or custom-made shower stalls made of tile, marble, or solid-surfacing slabs. Compared to plastic or fiberglass pans, the stone ones look and feel more substantial. Because shower pans are available in many colors, you'll easily find a match for your stall. There are three standard-shape prefabricated shower pans from which to choose: neoangle, square, and rectangular. The neoangle is a wise choice if you're trying to save floor space.

above This neoangle shower stall tucks neatly into a corner, a space-saving plus. For a stall with one or more open sides, order fixed, matching panels, which must be made of tempered glass, safety glass, wire glass, or plastic. Most door and side panel assemblies are about 70 inches high.

SHOWER extras

- **Soap dishes** and **storage shelves** are built into the walls of a prefabricated unit or added during the construction of a custom model.
- A **built-in or fold-down bench** makes foot washing easier and safer. It's a must for older people.
- **Grab bars** at a convenient height help when you step into and out of the stall.

Custom-Made Stalls

Compared to prefabricated stalls, custom-made shower stalls offer more options. You can match them to your space and to your design preference—whether a small room with multiple showerheads, an open stall with low walls, or a dramatic enclosure with a vaulted ceiling and skylights. A shower stall may be square or circular in shape.

Waterproof materials for the walls include tile, marble, granite, quartz surface or solid-surfacing, cast polymer, tempered glass, and glass block. To prevent leaking, make sure the shower pan is properly installed. A professional plumber or a tile setter can do the job to satisfaction.

Regarding doors and side panels, you have numerous choices in styles and configurations. If your stall is recessed, all you need is a door, with jambs and hardware for mounting. If your stall has one or more open sides, you can order fixed, matching panels made of tempered glass, safety glass, wire glass, or plastic. Etched-glass patterns are decorative, and frosted-glass panels offer privacy.

The frame that holds the door and panels can be finished in chrome, brass, bronze, white, black, or other decorator colors. A frameless, clear-glass enclosure has a nearly invisible effect.

A stall used as a steam bath requires a door and a top that seal tightly. This luxury requires a vapor barrier on the ceiling and wall framing to prevent steam from rotting the studs and joists. You'll also need a steam generator outside the shower; hire professionals to do the wiring and plumbing. (Some prefabricated shower stalls have a top and a door that seal tightly for a steam bath.)

Standard Pans

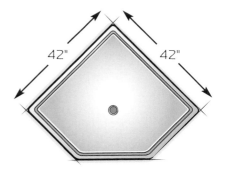

Neoangle pans are available up to 42 inches square.

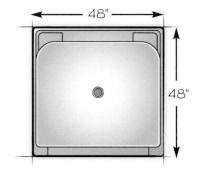

Square pans measure as large as 48 inches per side.

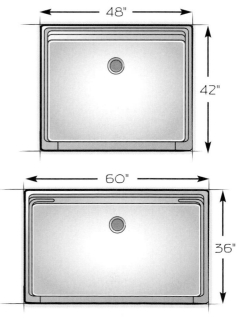

Rectangular pans come in several sizes. A rectangular pan can measure up to 60 inches wide.

Types of Tubs

Stand-alone tubs offer real bathing luxury. They're a great choice if you've got the necessary space to place them. Wear and tear is an important consideration. Will you be bathing splashing children; washing the dog; or taking a quiet soak?

There are numerous shapes, sizes, and materials from which to choose. Because of the plumbing, floor support, and logistical issues involved in installing a new tub, you want to make sure you get it right the first time.

Recessed/Alcove Tub

Reliable and typically no-frills, the alcove tub is still the most common tub type. It's enclosed on three sides and generally less expensive than a freestanding unit. This style is often used for tub/shower combinations. The faucets are typically wall-mounted. It's a good choice if you plan to install grab bars.

Corner Tubs

Made to stand alone or be fitted to the room, this tub is not typically used where a tub/shower combination is desired. Available in 5- or 6-foot lengths, it's similar to a recessed tub except for a finished side and end. It uses more floor space than some other models. However, one type of corner tub fits diagonally in the corner, providing a more open feeling than a standard unit. You can outfit a corner tub with drains on either side or in the middle.

Freestanding Tubs

Claw-foot: It's built on four legs; all sides of it are visible.
Pedestal: Oval in shape, it does not rest on feet but rather on an oval base. Handheld showerheads are often added to pedestal tubs. One advantage over claw-foot: You don't have to clean under a pedestal tub.

Drop-In or Platform Tubs

Floor-mounted sunken tubs are available, but they are very difficult to climb out of. That's why most drop-in tubs are mounted on a platform.

Whirlpool Tubs

A whirlpool tub gets its bubbling action from a water circulating system, with air mixed in. Most whirlpool baths have adjustable water jets that can target certain areas vigorously.

Tub and Shower Clearances

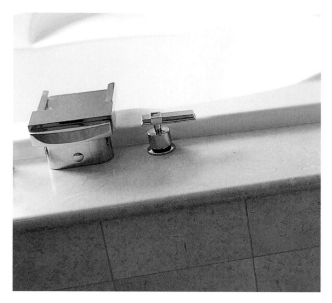

Tub Clearance

- If the tub is approached from the side, ensure a 30×60-inch area of clear floor space in front.
- If the tub has a head-on approach, plan for a 48×60-inch area of clear space.
- If possible, avoid steps leading into the tub area.
- Consider installing safety rails.

Tub Controls

- Make sure controls are accessible from both inside and outside the tub.
- The preferred height for the controls lies between the rim of the tub and 33 inches above the floor, and below any grab bar that is on the same wall.
- If separate hot and cold water controls are installed in a tub (this is not permissible in a shower stall), place the hot water control so that it is on the left when viewed from inside the tub.

Shower Clearance

- For showers less than 60 inches wide, clear floor space should be 36 inches deep and at least 12 inches wider than the shower.
- For showers wider than 60 inches, clear floor space should be 36 inches deep and at least the width of the shower.

Shower Interior

- At minimum, enclosed showers should have 34×34 inches of usable interior space, measured from wall to wall. If space permits, most people prefer a larger shower space. (In tight spaces, you might be able to manage 32×32 inches.)
- Water controls, grab bars, and fold-down seats don't reduce the measurement, but additional space is necessary when incorporating built-in seats or benches.
- Include a bench or seat at least 15 inches deep and located 17 to 19 inches above the floor. (You'll have to reinforce the shower wall.)
- Grab bars are recommended, with placement 33 to 36 inches above the floor.

Shower Controls

- Make sure controls are accessible from both inside and outside the shower.
- The preferred height for the controls is 38 to 48 inches above the floor and above any grab bar.
- A showerhead is typically installed 72 to 78 inches above the floor; 78 inches is ideal for a person who is 5 feet 8 inches tall, and 72 inches is recommended for a person who is 5 feet 4 inches tall.
- Adjustable, handheld showerheads are recommended; it's best to have the lowest position no higher than 48 inches above the floor.

Shower Entrance

- Shower doors should open out into the bathroom rather than into the stall.
- Avoid steps leading into the shower.
- Consider safety rails at the entrance.

Flooring

Choose flooring materials that are appropriate for how the room will be used. Bathrooms should be covered in durable materials such as hardwoods, nonslippery tile, natural stone, vinyl, indoor/outdoor carpeting, or laminate. For more information on flooring choices, see the shopping guide in Chapter Four, page 147.

Safety First

Safety is a primary concern when choosing bathroom flooring. Falls are dangerous for everyone but especially so for the elderly, children, and those who are physically challenged. The majority of slips and falls that occur inside households are caused by improper installation and maintenance of materials, a buildup of grease and grime, extensive wear, and the properties of the flooring material itself. You can avoid many accidents if you put the right flooring materials in the right places and properly maintain them. Some potentially slippery situations in bathrooms follow:

- Hard surfaces, which are often naturally slippery, especially when highly polished or naturally glossy.
- Water left puddled on a bathroom floor.
- Loose tiles or floorboards, as well as protruding nails or staples.
- Uneven transitions between rooms or types of flooring.
- Flooring material that visually obscures transitions between levels.
- Wooden floors that are not properly sanded and sealed. (They present the risk of splinters for bare feet.)

Least Slippery Flooring

The least slippery surfaces are rubber, textured surfaces, low-pile or indoor/outdoor carpet, surfaces with low-gloss or no-gloss finishes, and surfaces that absorb water. Even the safest surfaces must be properly installed, consistently cleaned, and well-maintained to ensure against accidents. Polished marble flooring in a bathroom can be dangerous.

Cleaning and Maintenance

Any flooring material will need cleaning and maintenance on a regular basis. Regular care lengthens the life of your floor, guarantees that warranties will be honored, and keeps the surface looking its best. Once the floor is in use, dirt, stains, scratches, and tears are inevitable. The longer the time between cleanings and repair, the worse the problem becomes.

above Safe and smooth transitions between rooms with different flooring materials are essential. Slight differences in height can cause stumbles and potentially dangerous falls.

How much are you willing to do? The amount of care a floor needs after installation and the amount of time you are willing to spend taking care of it are crucial design and planning considerations.

Maintenance requirements vary even among similar materials. Ceramic tile requires less maintenance than natural stone, which must be resealed and polished occasionally. Cork and hardwoods also require reapplication of sealers and finishes as they wear.

structural CONCERNS

New floors? Heavy tubs? Taking down walls? If you are replacing the floor, consider the weight of the new material you have selected and find out whether the floor structure can support the new flooring. Be careful with load-bearing walls; always consult a professional.

Lighting

A good lighting scheme combines ambient, task, and accent lighting. Ambient lighting provides general lighting for the whole room, eliminates shadows, and lights the floor for safety. Task lighting brightens up activity areas, such as sinks, showers, and vanities. The spillover from task lighting also contributes to overall lighting of the room. Accent lighting highlights special decorative or structural features.

The best combination of bulbs and fixtures varies with the size of the room and the style.

Ambient Lighting

The sources of ambient lighting are ceiling fixtures and natural light from windows and skylights. Recessed ceiling fixtures cause less glare than fixtures hanging from the ceiling. Use incandescent bulbs with recessed fixtures. The NKBA recommends 2½ to 4 watts of incandescent light per square foot or half of a watt of fluorescent light per square foot. However, other variables come into play. For example, the spread of light varies from fixture to fixture. The wider the spread, the fewer fixtures needed.

The combined surface areas of all windows and skylights in a bath should equal at least 10 percent of the square footage of the bath. To increase the amount of natural light, add another window. If window placement raises privacy issues, consider:

- Using semisheer window treatments that let in light while maintaining privacy.
- Installing glass block or prefabricated acrylic-block panels.
- Using glass with frosted-, etched-, or stained-glass panes.
- Installing a skylight, which lets in five times as much light as a window the same size.

Task Lighting

Good lighting is critical in the grooming/makeup vanity or dressing area. The goal of vanity lighting is to light the face of the user while preventing shadows. Ceiling-mounted fixtures alone will not do the trick in any size bathroom. At a minimum you also need a strip of incandescent lights above the mirror. Use wall-mounted fixtures, preferably with multiple bulbs arranged vertically at eye level on both sides of the mirror. Arrange fixtures so that light is directed from above and from both sides. Incandescent bulbs or fluorescent tubes cast a nice, warm glow.

In powder rooms and other small baths, a ceiling fixture and fixtures at the mirror usually provide adequate lighting, but larger baths require fixtures near the tub and shower, the toilet, and the vanity area. In the toilet area, a ceiling

above Sconces perform as both task and accent lights. They provide working light at the sink, and their unusual shades add style and focus to the setting. Natural light from exterior windows also functions as a lighting source during the day.

fixture with a 60- to 75-watt incandescent light or a 30- to 40-watt fluorescent tube is recommended. For tubs and showers, install enclosed vapor-proof (moisture-proof) light fixtures; 60 watts of incandescent illumination is recommended. Position light fixtures to avoid a glare in your eyes when you are soaking in the tub.

Consider using dimmer switches on fixtures with incandescent or dimmable fluorescent bulbs.

Accent Lighting

Accent lighting highlights decorative features. The light source needs to be about three times the intensity used for ambient lighting. You can use low-wattage halogen lights or a recessed light with an "eyeball" lens, a fitting that directs a point of light.

Ventilation

Bathrooms get steamy and wet. If your bath lacks proper ventilation, over time the humid conditions will encourage the growth of mold and mildew, which can lead to problems. Windows are, of course, a great source of ventilation, but a mechanical ventilation system that's capable of moving all the air from the bath to the outdoors eight times an hour is recommended. Every bathroom is well-served by a ventilation fan. Most such fans are mounted in the wall or ceiling and are vented to the outdoors.

Heating and Cooling

Do you need better heating and/or cooling in your new bath? A common problem is a bathroom that is too chilly to be comfortable, particularly when you're just stepping out of the shower on a winter morning.

Before the renovation, discuss with your professionals whether additional insulation or new windows would be a wise investment. Discuss this up front and make sure your final decision works into your budget and your final contract with your builder or designer.

You may also want to install auxiliary heat. Most additional heating sources in a bath are generated by electricity and are classified as either convection heat or radiant heat.

Convection heaters use a fan to force heated air from a wall- or ceiling-mounted source. They are a good source of general heat, as they distribute warmth quickly and evenly. Don't install them next to the bath or shower; fan-forced air, even when warm, feels uncomfortably cool on wet skin.

Radiant heat moves in waves. Sources of radiant heat include a heat lamp, baseboard heater, wall panel, or radiant floor heater. Radiant heating systems installed beneath the flooring are a popular choice because they're quiet and don't cause drafts. However, they may take longer to heat up the room, may require additional electrical circuits, and are more expensive to run. Some are available with timers so that you can have the heat come on before you get up in the morning.

In addition to adding a heat source, make sure the bath retains its heat. Reduce drafts in your bath by sealing air leaks and improving insulation, and consider buying new, improved windows.

Adapting Your Heating System

If your bathroom has always been cooler than preferred or you plan to enlarge it, you may be able to adapt your home's system to better suit your needs.

Forced hot-air systems distribute heat through a network of ducts and outlets, or registers. Adapting

don't forget
FANS

- Fans are rated by how many cubic feet per minute (cfm) of air they can move. Larger rooms need fans with higher cfm ratings.
- An easy way to calculate your bath's cfm requirement is to take the square footage of the bath and add 5 to it. For example, a 100-square-foot room would need a fan rated at 105 cfm or higher. If the square footage plus 5 gives you a number in between available fan ratings, choose the higher-rated fan.
- Sones are a measure of loudness. With sones, a higher rating means the fan is louder. One sone generates about the same noise as a refrigerator. Most homeowners will choose a fan that produces less than 3 sones at full speed.
- Properly installing a fan will reduce fan noise and increase efficiency. Rigid metal ducts are preferred over more flexible plastic.
- If your bath is sealed tight, the fan can't do its job. If possible, open a window after you take a shower. It's also a good idea to leave an inch of space at the bottom of the bathroom door. This enables the fan to draw in fresh air.
- Other options to discuss with your professional builder include heat recovery ventilators and exterior-mounted ventilation fans.

the system involves extending ductwork and adding registers. Most systems can accommodate one or two outlets without changes to the furnace. Place the registers in spots where they won't blow against people using the toilet, getting out of the shower, or standing in front of the vanity. In colder climates, registers should be closer to the floor to allow heat to spread through the room as it rises. In warmer climates, where the system is more often used for air-conditioning, outlets should be higher on the wall.

Forced hot-water, or hydronic, systems distribute hot water through a network of pipes. The pipes supply the room's heating units (radiators, fan-coil units, or convectors). A second set of pipes returns cooled water to the boiler. If space is tight, install a baseboard convector along the toe-kick of the vanity or a fan-powered coil system on the ceiling.

Electrical-resistance systems use baseboard heaters or wall panels to convert electric current into heat. Each room is heated independently, allowing more flexibility and precise control over room temperature. To heat up your bathroom, you can install an additional heater. And if adapting a forced hot-air or hot-water system proves too difficult, disruptive, or costly, adding an electrical-resistance heater may be an alternative.

Cooling Down

When a ventilation fan doesn't cool your bathroom, it may be time for a room air-conditioner, which runs independently and is easy to install. However, it can be noisy and make the room less attractive.

If you have a central forced-air heating system in your home, consider adding a central air-conditioning system. Although it's a costly option, redoing the bath may give you a reason to finally have a system installed. Central air-conditioning is quieter than a room unit, and the cooling unit stays out of sight.

Avoid placing a ceiling fan in the bathroom. The force of moving air against wet skin is uncomfortable.

---

what about HEAT LAMPS ?

Some heat lamps are designed with a fan and a light and provide radiant or convection heat. Not meant to heat large areas, they work best when installed to provide spot heating, such as by a tub or shower or above a vanity. Heat lamps are easier to install than other heating sources and work well in small baths. The ceiling location also eliminates the possibility of bumping the heater and getting burned, as can happen with a baseboard heater.

A heat lamp is installed in much the same way as a recessed downlight. If your ceiling is insulated, you'll have to install a fireproof barrier for the fixture. A heat lamp can be wired to a timer so that you wake up to a cozy shower stall or vanity area on cold mornings.

Not all heat lamps are designed for bathroom use. Check product specifications before installing one.

Plumbing and Electrical Issues

With any major bath remodeling project, it pays to invest in quality plumbing, wiring, heating, venting, and air-conditioning. Don't look for ways to scrimp or cut costs. Take advantage of the time that the walls, ceilings, and floors will be open and decide what investments need to be made, where to add extra outlets, and what extras will accommodate future plans you may have. **Don't be afraid to consult professionals if you have questions.** (You must meet all building codes, which is particularly important when dealing with electrical and plumbing systems.)

Plumbing

Here are major plumbing issues to be aware of:
- Will you be moving the sink and/or adding a second sink? If yes, water pipes and drains will have to be moved and expenses will increase.
- Significant plumbing considerations (and costs) will arise if you install fixtures in new locations. Even if you aren't moving fixtures, this is still a good time to have your pipes inspected and replaced if needed. It's always easier to do when the walls are down.
- Local codes are there to promote safe and efficient operation of your home's basic system. They should be followed not only because they are logical and grounded in experience, but because you can pay stiff fines and lose valuable time if you don't pass required inspections.

- No floor joists should be cut to route pipes to the vertical stack. This is to maintain the structural integrity of the floor.
- A whirlpool tub may need its own separate hot-water tank and electrical circuit. If your plan includes a new tub or whirlpool, the floor may have to be reinforced. Also, will you be able to get the new whirlpool or shower unit through the doorway? Don't forget to check!

Electrical

The bathroom requires at least two 120-volt circuits. One is a 15-amp general lighting circuit. It supplies power to lights and to an exhaust vent fan. The second is a 20-amp circuit that supplies power to a GFCI (ground fault circuit interrupter) receptacle.
- To guard against electrical shock, all bathroom receptacles, lights, and switches must be protected with GFCIs because of the proximity to water.
- Panels for mechanical, electrical, and plumbing systems should be easily accessible.
- Make sure you have enough outlets in the bath. Duplex receptacles are typically needed near each sink. Outlets inside cabinets offer a handy way to charge and store certain appliances. Don't forget outlets for vacuum cleaners, televisions, clocks, music systems or radios, and towel warmers.

Creating a Floor Plan

frequently asked LAYOUT QUESTIONS

Can't somebody else do the drawings?
Drawings can be prepared by designers at home centers, architects, and interior designers, but it's helpful to map the space and have some ideas before you meet with a pro. Better preparation means more productive work sessions.

What if I'm doing it all myself?
If you will be actively involved in the construction phase, then your drawings are much more critical and must be very accurate. Numerous online tools are available. Have your drawings checked by professionals, and comply with all local codes.

What if I'm not moving fixtures?
With many bathroom remodeling and renovation projects, the homeowners choose to leave the tub, sink, and toilet where they are, a decision that greatly reduces the cost. If that is your plan, you probably don't need to go to all the trouble of drawing floor plans and elevation views, but you will still need to measure and consult with a professional.

What's the difference between a floor plan and an elevation?
A floor plan is an overhead view of the entire space on one piece of paper. This is the view that best shows the layout and traffic patterns, window and door placement, and locations of fixtures and cabinetry and fixed objects. An elevation view is drawn from the perspective of one looking directly at an interior wall. It indicates scale and proportions, but it is a two-dimensional drawing and will not show perspective. Separate elevation drawings of each wall are required. Studying the elevation views can also uncover potential clearance problems.

What tools do I need to get started?
A 50-foot tape measure (recommended) and a stepladder. You also need ¼-inch graph paper, tracing paper, a notepad, pencils, a scale (architect's) ruler, and erasers. Recruit a helper for measuring; the results will be far more accurate.

Starting the Layout Process

Most people remodeling a bathroom leave the toilet, sink, tub, and shower where they are because a renovation is far less expensive if major plumbing doesn't have to be rerouted. But if you're putting a bath in a new space or if your current bath just doesn't work, there are three options for developing a layout. You can do the layout by hand, hire an architect, or take advantage of a computer design program.

Floor Plan by Computer

Computer design programs have replaced most of the hard work involved in laying out a bathroom. Most home centers have computers available that will create floor plans and elevations from dimensions you provide (or they will measure the space for you). There is also software available commercially, but not all of it is compatible with every computer.

Not only will the program develop plans, it will build a three-dimensional rendering so that you can take a virtual tour of the space.

No matter what method you use to develop a layout, you must still measure the room accurately and at least create a rough sketch of the space.

Floor Plan by Hand

Following is the order of work for laying out a bathroom floor plan by hand. It requires only a tape measure, pencil, ruler, and graph paper.

- Start by measuring the space. Then draw an overhead floor plan of the room and add your measurements.
- Place the fixtures—toilet, sink and vanity, tub, and shower stall—one by one. As you add each element, subtract the wall space it occupies from the amount available to make sure everything will fit.

The National Kitchen and Bath Association (NKBA) has developed guidelines that help create the safest and most comfortable bathrooms, and your installation must meet national and local building codes. When you plan your bath meet as many guidelines as you can—but even the NKBA says it can be difficult to meet them all. In this chapter, they are grouped into five sidebars and presented as they come up in the process so they can be easily followed. Once you're done, take your plans to a designer and then to a building inspector for input.

How to Measure

Most experts recommend that you draw your floor plan in two stages; begin with a rough sketch and later refine it, making it a more precise scale drawing of your space.

Draw a **rough outline** of your bathroom on graph paper, marking off windows, doors, toilets, bathtubs, and other fixed elements. If you would like to enlarge the area, note any adjacent space that you might consider for expansion.

- Start at the corners and measure the length and width of the bath. It's OK to round off the dimensions and measurements to the nearest ½ inch. (For the final drawings, it is better to be more precise and round up to the nearest ⅛ inch.)
- The next step is to measure the spaces between all the elements you have noted. Be sure to record all the measurements on your drawing as you proceed. It's best to measure in inches (rather than feet and inches).
- Verify that the individually recorded measurements/distances along each wall add up to the total length you recorded. Also make sure the total measurements of opposite walls are equal. If not, check your work.
- Draw an elevation view of each wall in the bath. To do this, measure the height of the ceilings, doors, windows, cabinets, and other such elements. If there is a vaulted ceiling or varying ceiling heights, note this.

Drafting to Scale

To prepare detailed drawings you need to decide on the scale (inches to feet on the drawing) that will properly represent the details you need. For larger bathrooms start with a scale of ½-inch on paper equals 1 foot in the room. For smaller bathrooms, you might want to start with a scale of 1 inch on paper equals 1 foot in the room.

To double-check for accuracy, remeasure the outside dimensions of the room, the openings, doors and windows, interior wall thicknesses (measured at the doorways), and all other fixed elements. Mark the locations and dimensions of outlets and switches, pipes (hot- and cold-water lines and drainage lines), gas lines, and vent ducts. For outlets, for example, measure the distance from the left-hand corner of the wall the outlet is on to the center of the cover plate. Also measure the distance between the center of the cover plate and the floor.

Create a Final Floor Plan

One easy way to use this base floor plan drawing is to make several photocopies, then experiment with different layouts and configurations. Another popular approach is to use tracing paper. You can trace the walls with changes you are considering, then try various ways to fit the shower, tub, toilet, etc., into new locations. Because you're not writing on the actual floor plan, you can do this as many times as you wish. Refer to the NKBA and other space guidelines on the following pages while you work through various options. And remember the details, such as space needed for doors and drawers. Using movable templates that represent cabinets and fixtures can also be helpful.

For a more detailed look at how to draft a final floor plan, see pages 111 through 114.

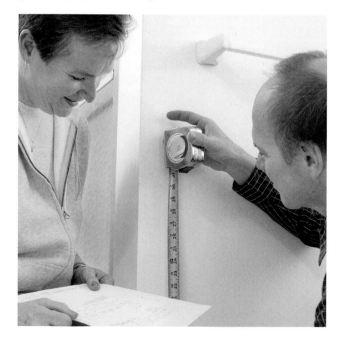

A Sample Bathroom Floor Plan

Even in this age of standardization, no two bathrooms are quite the same dimensions, but basic principles of layout and design will guide you through the process and allow you to make everything fit properly into the space. The sample layout that unfolds on the following pages is based on an average-size bathroom and includes the most sought after elements: a double-sink vanity, a shower stall, a bathtub, and a toilet.

NKBA guidelines are included along the way to help you make decisions about functionality and safety.

❶ Outline the Floor Plan

Choose a scale for your drawing (here, one square of graph paper equals 6 square inches of actual wall space). Measure all four walls of your bathroom. Measure the doors and windows, including the trim, as part of the overall size. Using your dimensions, draw the walls to scale and place the windows and doors. Number the walls (there are four in this example). Wall 4 has a window; the doorway is on Wall 1.

In this example, Walls 2 and 4 are 144 inches long; Walls 1 and 3 are 112 inches. The doorway on Wall 1 is 36 inches wide, including trim. The window on Wall 4 is 30 inches wide, including trim. For an existing bath, mark plumbing lines and drains that won't be moved. Also mark the outlets, switches, and vents.

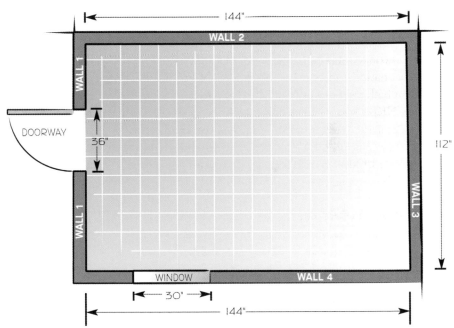

❷ Place the Toilet

Start with the toilet because it requires the most clearance. Here, the toilet is on Wall 2, 1 inch away from the wall. You need a clearance of 16 inches from the center of the toilet to Wall 3 and another 16 inches on the other side of the toilet. You also need 48×48 inches of clear space in front of the toilet. In this example, the clear space begins at the wall, putting the center of the clear space—and the toilet—24 inches from the wall. For comfort, you'll want at least another 16 inches between the center of the toilet and the edge of the adjacent fixture. Adding it all up, the adjacent fixture—whatever it is—will have to be at least 40 inches from the wall.

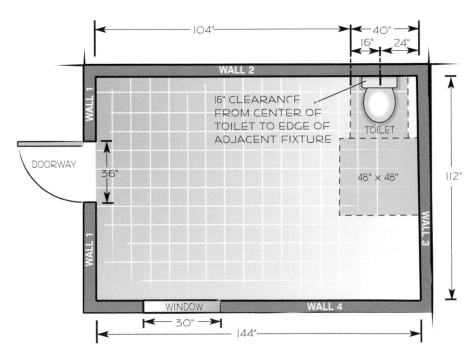

space requirements: **TOILETS**

The NKBA guidelines for toilet design include the following:

- Allow at least 16 inches of clearance on each side of the centerline of the toilet to any obstruction, fixture, or equipment.

- If space is tight, reduce the clearance to 15 inches. Reducing the clearance may make the toilet less comfortable.

- Install the toilet paper holder within reach of a person seated on the toilet. The ideal location is slightly in front of

the edge of the toilet bowl (about 8 inches), approximately 26 inches above the floor.

- If you install a toilet in a separate compartment it should be at least 36 inches wide and 66 inches long. Install a swing-out door or a pocket door on the opening. Make the door opening at least 32 inches wide. All of these dimensions will have to be larger in a barrier-free bathroom.

If you are replacing the toilet but not changing the location, note the rough-in (distance from the wall to the drain) to select a proper replacement.

③ **Place the Sink and Vanity**

First decide whether you want storage space at the sink. If not, consider a freestanding sink. If you want storage, include a sink and vanity. Next decide whether you want one sink or two. If all you need is one, layout is simple. Draw a 22-inch-deep counter in the available space on Wall 2 and put the sink anywhere along the counter. For comfort, leave 15 inches between the center of the sink and any wall to the side. As a practical matter, most people center them on the vanity. If you want two sinks, place the sinks at each end of the vanity. To allow enough elbow room, position the sinks so that the centers are at least 30 inches apart.

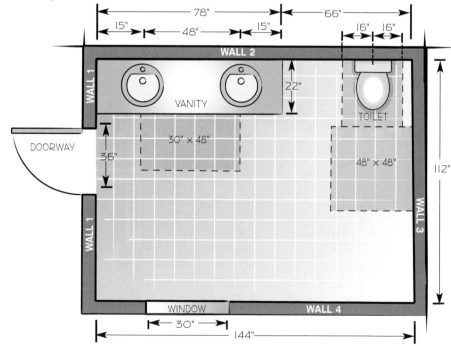

space requirements: **VANITIES**

A two-sink vanity won't work if users are competing for space. Here are some guidelines that give everyone enough elbow room. The guidelines are based on standards developed by the NKBA. Remember: They're guidelines, not rules.

- If you're including two vanities, make them different heights so that different people can use them. One of them can be a dressing table with knee space for sitting.
- Locate a mirror above a vanity so that its bottom edge is no more than 40 inches above the floor. If the top of the mirror is tilted away from the wall, its bottom edge can be 48 inches above the floor.
- Leave at least 15 inches of clearance from the centerline of a sink to the closest sidewall.
- If you're including two sinks in a vanity, leave at least 30 inches of clearance between the centerline of each. If the sinks are wider than 30 inches, increase the distance to provide enough elbow room.
- Consider door size and drawer width when designing a vanity. Get split doors in cabinets that are 24 inches or wider. Large single doors can be awkward to open, especially in a narrow bathroom. You also should avoid narrow doors and drawers. Nine- and 12-inch widths can be too narrow to be useful. Don't simply divide an available space in half when designing cabinetry. For example, if you divide a 54-inch space into two 27-inch-wide units, each one would need at least two doors. If you divide the space into cabinets 18 and 36 inches wide, you would need only three doors. Cabinet runs with fewer doors and larger openings are better than ones with more doors and smaller openings.
- To eliminate sharp corners, use countertops with rounded or clipped corners and eased edges.

➍ Place the Tub

Tubs come in many sizes. This one is 36 inches wide and 72 inches long. But placing it isn't just a matter of determining whether there's enough space along the wall. You also have to make sure there's enough space to get in and out. You need a clear floor area of 30×60 inches. The required floor areas in front of two fixtures can overlap. If the clear floor space in your layout overlaps a fixture, however, you have a potential problem. Move the templates around on your floor plan to find an arrangement that works better. Or reconsider the size of fixtures; changing the length of a vanity or tub, for example, may free up the space you want. If it doesn't and this is new construction, you may want to design a larger space.

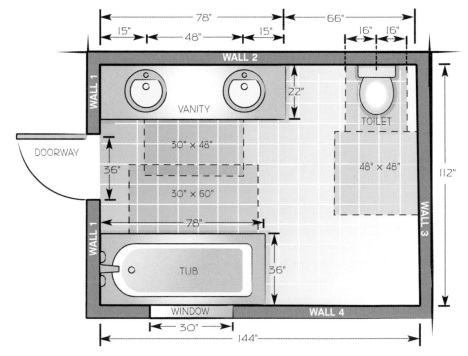

space requirements: **TUBS**

When you're planning your tub, a few guidelines will make it safer and easier to use:

■ Install safety rails to make it easy to get in and out of the tub. Steps, on the other hand, are dangerous.

■ If you're putting a showerhead in the bathtub, install a pressure-balancing/temperature regulator or a temperature-limiting device to prevent scalding.

■ You can install a handheld showerhead instead of a fixed one. To make sure all users can reach the showerhead, install it so that its lowest position is no higher than 48 inches from the floor.

■ For convenience, install controls so that they're accessible from both inside and outside the tub. Locate the controls between the rim and 33 inches above the floor. Make sure the controls are below any grab bar on the same wall. Offset the controls toward the room, between the showerhead and the tub rim.

■ If you install separate hot- and cold-water controls in a bathtub, make sure the hot water control is on the left when facing the control from inside the tub.

■ Install only safety glass—laminated glass with a plastic interlayer—for any glass tub enclosure or partition that is within 18 inches of the floor.

⑤ Place the Shower

This bath has a tub and a shower stall. The stall is a 36-inch-square model with an angled glass door at the corner. (Designers call this a neoangle stall.)

Because all other main elements are already in place, the shower can go only two places. One is along Wall 3; the other is in the corner formed by Walls 3 and 4. In choosing between them, plan for the 36×48-inch clear floor space you'll want in front of the shower. The clear space can overlap any other clear space, but when a clear space overlaps a fixture, it shrinks by the size of the fixture. If you want enough clear space, the stall can only go where it's shown.

Having settled on putting the shower stall in the corner, however, you do have a choice about where the door should go. It can face the toilet, or the shower can be a neoangle stall with the door on the corner, as shown.

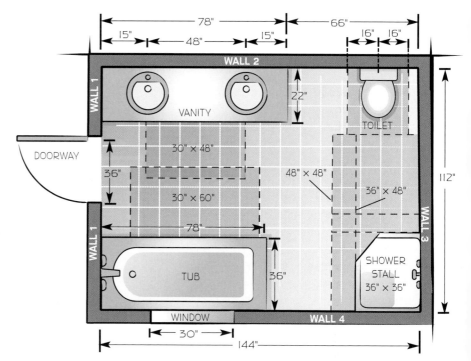

space requirements: **SHOWERS**

The NKBA guidelines for shower design include:

- Interior dimensions of an enclosed shower should provide 34×34 inches of usable interior space. Grab bars, controls, and movable and folding seats don't reduce the measurement, but built-in seats do. You can settle for 32×32, but this may make the shower uncomfortable for some users.
- A bench should be 17 to 19 inches above the floor and at least 15 inches deep. It can be solid, hanging, or folding.
- Shower doors should open into the bathroom—not the stall.
- To reduce the risk of falls, avoid installing steps.
- Install a pressure-balancing/temperature regulator or a temperature-limiting device for the showerhead to prevent scalding.
- Shower controls should be accessible from inside and outside the stall, 38 to 48 inches above the floor, and above the grab bar if there is one. Locate the controls between the showerhead and the stall door. Install a handheld showerhead, 48 inches above the floor in its lowest position.
- Install laminated safety glass with a plastic interlayer, tempered glass, or approved plastic for any clear face of a shower enclosure or partition that is within 18 inches of the floor.

kid **SAFE**

With all baths, but especially children's, homeowners must pay attention to safety, durability, and adaptability. Here are some key points:

- Use slip-resistant materials on floors and other surfaces.
- Avoid multiple levels in a bath or steps to the tub.
- Make sure no lighting fixture is placed within the reach of a person seated or standing in the tub or shower area.
- Use only those receptacles, lights, and switches that are protected with ground fault circuit interrupters (GFCIs).
- Include a seat or bench in your shower.
- Cover exposed pipes.
- Use night-lights to illuminate the hallway to the bathroom and the room itself.
- Install privacy locks that you can easily open in the event of an emergency.
- Use soap dispensers in the shower.
- Install outlet safety covers.
- Install childproof latches and locks.
- Install safety covers over sharp vanity/countertop corners, the tub spout, and other sharp areas.
- Install towel hooks at "kid height."
- Use only unbreakable drinking glasses in the bath area.
- Have a child-safe step stool nearby or perhaps install a built-in step stool by the sink.
- Check your home's water heater and set it to no higher than 120°F.
- Install a tub and shower pressure-balancing/temperature regulator or a temperature-limiting device to prevent scalding.
- Don't install heated towel bars in baths used by small children.
- Never leave young children unattended in the bathroom; small amounts of standing water and toilets present drowning hazards (toilet lid locks are available).
- Keep medicines and cleaning supplies out of the reach of children.

Money Matters

A key part of the planning phase is to establish a detailed construction budget. This involves documenting what you are willing to spend, calculating an estimate of how much your planned renovation or addition will cost, and determining if the two are in line with each other.

As you move through the process, you will minimize problems and headaches by keeping (and following!) a detailed budget. Make sure your selection of fixtures and other elements and the cost of each are documented in your contract. Tracking costs all the way through will help you know if there are places where you will need to modify your wish list in order to stay on budget.

Detailed estimates, including materials and labor breakdowns, help you set priorities and make trade-offs as necessary. After you develop a realistic budget, it's good practice to plan for an overrun of about 12 percent. Planning for that at the beginning of the project can help prevent a real money crunch (and headache) later.

Be Prepared for Anything

Construction costs vary significantly by region.
- Always be prepared for the unexpected. Surprises can pop up any time you open a wall or cut into a floor, especially in older homes where structural or mechanical problems are more likely to be lurking.
- Changing the position of plumbing pipes and fixtures significantly increases your costs.

Is the Timing Right?

Before jumping into your remodeling project, go through this checklist and make an honest evaluation of whether sinking money into a major project for your home at this particular time is a smart financial move.
- How old is your home?
- How long have you lived in your home?
- How long do you think you'll stay in your home?
- Have others in your neighborhood undertaken remodeling projects?

If resale value is a key consideration, it will influence design and product selections you make. You will have to gear the look toward the mainstream, which may not mesh with your personal tastes. Do some research on your neighborhood, as if you were a newcomer moving into the area. Investigate the schools, drive around and see how property is being maintained, research real estate values, and talk with an agent to get a feel for how much of your investment you might be able to recoup if you later sell your home. Resale value may not be a key consideration, but it's better to do your research.

above Accurate estimates from contractors will help you prepare a budget that you can keep.

Budget Reducers

Consider compromises that will save you money without sacrificing the overall plan. You can often get the same designer look for a smaller price tag. Talk with your designer or other professional, look through magazines, browse home centers, or shop for closeout models or discounted materials.
- Do you really need a full-blown expansion? Would a major makeover, layout change, or bump-out do the trick at a much smaller cost?
- Do you need to change the location of the plumbing or electricity?
- Do you really need two sinks?
- Would a half-wall provide the desired level of privacy and a jazzy additional storage nook?
- Can you do some of the work yourself?

How to Pay

Some homeowners choose to save for a major project and pay for it without taking out a loan. Others take out a home equity loan, home equity line of credit, second mortgage, or take advantage of home centers that offer deferred billing and payments with no interest over proscribed time periods. While researching your options, go online; many websites will walk you through various scenarios. Talk with several different banks and mortgage companies or try a credit union if you are a member.

Finally, a major renovation is a significant expense and deserves the same consideration you'd give other major expenditures. Do not develop your budget and ways to pay for the project in isolation; make it a part of your overall financial planning (which often includes big-ticket items such as saving for retirement and college funds).

Budgeting Your Bathroom

Remodeling a bathroom costs, on average, $7,000 to $20,000. The first step in budgeting is making a good guess of what kind of bath project you have in mind. This means determining whether you are planning a spruce-up job, a change in layout, or an actual expansion or complete renovation. Remember that average project costs vary significantly by region, and the quality of the professionals you hire and materials you choose will determine your price point.

You can accomplish a minor fix-up with impressive cosmetic changes for a few thousand dollars, but a luxury expansion or redo costs $40,000 to $50,000 or more. Before you begin the actual interviewing process, have some informal discussions with contractors or local real estate agents to get a feel for costs and the features that are most popular among new home buyers. Many websites also provide a wealth of information about remodeling.

Watch out for extras. Sometimes to get the right look and features, you have to buy high-end products, but often cost is driven by extras you may not need or even want. Shop carefully!

PRIORITIZE
your options

For most bath renovations, a large part of the expense goes toward running new plumbing lines, replacing windows, and building new walls. If any of these are part of your plan, consider them fixed costs. After that, organize your wish list into the following categories: fixtures, cabinetry, and surfaces. Work back through your checklist and decide what is most important to you. Maybe the thought of relaxing in a whirlpool was enticing, but in reality you'd get more use out of a shower with all the bells and whistles. A fireplace may be over-the-top for your budget, but a cozy sitting area with your favorite books and an overstuffed chair might provide the soothing comfort you seek. Imagine a nook with a coffee station, music system, and small television: everything you need to turn this into that private getaway, that place that is yours alone. Go through each item on your wish list and then decide.

Average Costs

The following list of average costs may be useful as you start to build your budget. This list reflects estimated costs for the elements—it does not include installation costs. Remember that these are rough estimates, and price ranges vary by region. After using this information in the very preliminary stages, you can secure detailed price information by visiting stores; shopping online; and talking with builders, designers, and home center salespeople. When it comes to finalizing your budget, the only way to ensure an accurate and complete picture is to get bids and estimates from professionals.

Bathroom Sinks
Basic: $50–$150 (for acrylic)
Mid-range: $150–$400
High-end: $400–$3,000
Upgrades offer freestanding pedestals; solid-surfacing, stone, or exotic materials; consoles and table units; art-glass basins.

Sink Faucets
Basic: $60–$100 (a basic chrome two-handle faucet)
Mid-range: $100–$300 (brass, chrome, nickel, or other similar faucet)
High-end: $300–$1,000
The more expensive choices have nicer finishes, single-lever controls, and features such as motion sensors operation.

Toilets
Basic: $100–$200 (a traditional white two-piece toilet)
Mid-range: $200–$600
High-end: $700–$1,400
The more expensive toilets typically offer more color and style choices, use higher-grade porcelain, or are one-piece or pressure-assisted flush models.

Bathtubs, Including Whirlpools
Basic: $100–$150 (a standard 5–foot tub; fiberglass or enameled steel)
Mid-range: $150–$700
High-end: $700–$5,000
The more expensive tubs include options such as heavier materials, numerous colors, tub/shower combinations, unusual shapes, larger sizes, and whirlpools. (The more expensive whirlpools include features such as digital controls, a variable-speed pump, a separate hot-water heater, and maximum jets.)

Shower Enclosures

Basic: $100–$200 (freestanding aluminum shower stall)
Mid-range: $200–$1,000 (such as a 36-inch acrylic or fiberglass shower)
High-end: $1,000–$4,000

With the more expensive items, you will see options such as larger units (acrylic and angled); solid-surfacing shower walls; built-in ledges, benches, and shelving; and multihead shower systems.

Bathtub/Shower Faucet

Basic: $75–$100 (basic spout; fixed showerhead)
Mid-range: $200–$500
High-end: $500–$1,500 or more

The more expensive choices include adjustable-height, handheld, combination fixed/handheld showerheads, and multiple spray nozzles.

Flooring

Flooring is usually sold by the square foot. Prices vary widely among materials, among suppliers, and the cost of installation.

---

avoid budget NIGHTMARES

Most projects will go over budget, but with careful planning (including adding in ample fudge room), you shouldn't be hit with too many surprises.
Problems often occur when homeowners:

- Take the lowest bid without checking references.
- Change their minds halfway through the project.
- Fail to specify brand and model names in the contract which may result in larger expenses for higher-end items.
- Are informed that major structural defects were discovered during the demolition phase.

Meet the Pros

Design and Planning Phase

- Architects are certified by the American Institute of Architects. They work with you from the beginning and draw up all of the plans and specifications. They also will review plans that have been prepared by others. If you are planning a major addition, an architect can help ensure it works with the style of your home.
- Certified kitchen and bath designers must pass an exam to be certified by the NKBA (National Kitchen and Bath Association) and must fulfill continuing education requirements. They are qualified to produce layouts and review plans prepared by other professionals. They can help supervise the contractor's work. In home centers, certified designers work with clients and supervise other employees in the design area.
- Interior designers are qualified to provide planning and help in selecting materials, fixtures, elements, and colors. They can review plans and formulate design concepts. Some interior designers have a degree in interior design and are members of the American Society of Interior Designers. Some states also require that they be certified by the National Council of Interior Design.

Construction Phase

- General contractors oversee the entire job. General contractors will also hire and manage subcontractors who will do specific work such as plumbing or electrical installation, and they will get the correct building permits, schedule necessary inspections, and ensure compliance with local building codes. Contractors often offer design services as well. Hiring an experienced and reliable contractor is a critical step, especially if you're not using a designer.
- Design and build firms offer both design and general contracting services. These firms typically have designers or architects on staff and also serve as building contractors. Going this route can eliminate some of the headache of coordinating the activities and responsibilities of the various professionals involved in a major project.
- In addition to offering professional design services, most home centers will also work with you to arrange for the installation of many of the products you can purchase from them. Unlike many independent contractors that may take multiple "progress" payments over the course of the job, home centers may require full payment up front. However, the major home centers have every incentive to stand by their product and service offerings because the success of their businesses depends upon satisfied customers and positive word of mouth.

Consulting Professionals

If you need help planning and executing your project, hiring professionals is probably the answer. The type of pro you choose depends on what you need. Hire professionals only after looking carefully into credentials, experience, and what associations they belong to. Certification and membership in professional organizations may signify commitment, but other professionals may be just as or more competent.

The True Tests

The true tests of any designer or contractor are a portfolio of work, an interview to see if there's a good fit, good word of mouth, and excellent references from satisfied clients.
Before you begin consider the following:
- Are you really ready to start building? Have you thought through your dreams for your new bath and settled on a design plan? A contractor will not be able to make an accurate estimate without a plan.
- Some contractors give rough estimates and provide initial consultations for free. Others are reluctant to give ballpark estimates in case their true bid is higher.
- Make sure you can make payments as they come due.
- See what adjustments may need to be made to your homeowner's policy during the construction phase and to cover the added value of the work being done.
- Make sure your new bathroom will be compatible with all the other systems in your home such as HVAC (heating, ventilation, air-conditioning), plumbing, and wiring. It may be worth an inspection by a qualified professional.

COMMUNICATION
is key

- After the work is under way visit the site as often as possible without becoming an annoyance. Establishing a good relationship with the contractor and the crew will inevitably pay off.
- Leave a notebook in a designated spot that you and the crew use to write notes, questions, and comments for each other.
- Have weekly review meetings with the contractor and the on-site supervisor. Address any concerns immediately. Speak up if the work is not satisfactory, if people who were not designated in the contract are working on-site, or if something does not seem right to you.
- Good communication involves both listening and speaking out.

Get Recommendations

Be prepared to get bids for the job from at least three contractors and compare them carefully before you choose.
- Everybody has contacts for referrals, so don't be afraid to ask friends, relatives, neighbors, business colleagues, real estate agents, and bankers for referrals.
- Ask at home improvement centers.
- Ask trade professionals who have provided good service in your home.
- Look for job site signs in your neighborhood and find out how the site is managed and cleaned up on a daily basis.
- Ask the designer or architect you are working with to recommend general contractors.
- Contact your local Better Business Bureau; check with national trade associations (including the National Association of Home Builders Remodelers Council, the National Association of the Remodeling Industry, and, for architect referrals, the American Institute of Architects) for local members.

What About a Contract?

Contracts are essential. You can consult an attorney or you can find sample contracts online or at office supply stores. The contract must include a payment schedule, the start and completion dates, a detailed materials list, the total cost of the job, how you and the contractor will deal with changes, a warranty on materials and workmanship for one year, a request for lien release forms from the contractor and all the subcontractors on acceptance of final payment, and an arbitration clause in case there are problems that can't be resolved through negotiation.

No matter who you choose to complete your installation, review your contract carefully so that you can be confident of the product and workmanship warranties and other guarantees that come with your purchase.

Payment Schedule

Spell out the total price of the job and the payment schedule. If full payment is required up front, make sure you review the contract carefully and understand the extent of guarantees and warranties on products, installation, and materials. Otherwise, schedule a minimum of three payments. Pay 25 to 50 percent on signing, and make a second payment approximately halfway through the project. You could also make payments fixed to completion of phases. Always keep at least 20 percent of the total until the work is completed and you are completely satisfied.

Shopping Guide

Vanities, showers, toilets, faucets—there are hundreds of products that provide service in a bathroom, so how do you make the right choices? This shopping guide will point you toward what's right for you.

Shopping for the products that will realize your bathroom design should be a thorough and careful process. Plan for plenty of shopping time as you schedule your remodel so you'll be able to make informed decisions about both style and function in your new bathroom.

CHAPTER 4 CONTENTS

left Choosing the right fixtures and faucets is a major part of putting a bathroom together, but you must also consider accessories such as towel racks and soap holders to complete the design.

Sinks

Sinks are available in numerous shapes, with the most common shapes being rectangular, oval, round, and asymmetrical. Many materials are now available, but the most popular choices continue to be stainless steel and cast iron. Pick the right sink(s) for your bath by carefully considering:

- The purpose of the bath
- The available space
- Whether your bath will have one or more sinks
- Your design preferences
- The design features of other key fixtures and elements you are selecting
- Your budget

above Solid-surfacing counters with integrated sinks make cleanup and maintenance easy.

Vanity-Mounted Sinks

Drop-In Sinks

The most common vanity sinks are drop-in sinks. A self-rimming sink, a type of drop-in sink, fits into a hole that has been cut out in the countertop. The rolled edges of the sink sit on the countertop, and the joint between the rim of the sink and the countertop is caulked. A self-rimming sink can be used with almost any type of available countertop material, and it can be replaced without moving the countertop or pipes. However, the joint between the sink and the countertop requires regular cleaning.

Undermount Sinks

An undermount sink also is part of a vanity. It sits below the countertop and, when installed, is attached to the underside of the sink cutout in the countertop. It's easier to clean the countertop surrounding an undermount sink as opposed to a self-rimming or rimmed sink. Undermount sinks must be used with materials that are waterproof from both sides, such as solid-surfacing, quartz surfacing, granite, and other stones. Laminate countertops cannot be used with an undermount sink.

Integral Sinks

When a sink is part of the countertop material, it is called an integral sink. That is, the sink is molded from the same material to create an integral unit, with no visible joint between the sink and the counter. Possible materials include solid-surfacing, stainless steel, and stones. An easily cleaned surface, an integral sink provides a contemporary, clean look. If damaged, however, the entire piece must be replaced.

Vessel Sinks

A vessel sink is a bowl mounted on top of the countertop. It makes a bold design statement and probably is best reserved for an elegant powder room that doesn't get heavy traffic. It is common to see wall-mounted fixtures with a vessel sink.

Wall-Hung Sinks

The wall-hung variety is most often recommended in a universal design bath.

Unlike vanity sinks, there is typically no storage available beneath a wall-hung sink, and there is little or no countertop space. Some designs leave the plumbing exposed under the sink. If you have a family member who uses a wheelchair, be sure to cover the plumbing and rough surfaces with a protective material.

Unless the sink is for a powder room, make sure you plan a spot for toothbrushes, soap dishes, and other toiletries. Don't forget to consider the type of use your new bath will see and the cleaning required for different styles.

Wall-hung sinks work well in smaller spaces as do pedestal-style or corner drop-in sinks.

above A wall-mounted vessel sink makes a dramatic statement in this bathroom.

Freestanding Sinks

There are also several categories of freestanding sinks. From a contemporary console to an old-fashioned white pedestal sink, freestanding styles bring flair and style to any bathroom.

Console Sinks

A console sink is similar in look and function to a pedestal sink but has either two or four legs and a "tabletop" surrounding the bowl, offering more countertop space.

Pedestal Sinks

A pedestal sink is supported by a narrow base and is often used in a powder room, making the space appear larger.

Sink Materials (For general cost comparisons see page 117.)

Material	Description	Advantages	Disadvantages	Care
Stainless steel	The quality varies according to the gauge and nickel content, with the better styles being thicker and having a combination of nickel and chrome	• Available in a variety of sizes and shapes • Lightweight, durable, and corrosion resistant • Moderate price • Popular for contemporary bathrooms	• Shiny surface shows fingerprints, scratches, and water spots (brushed finishes show fewer marks) • Thin steel dents easily and shows scratches	• Easy to clean • Thinner gauges are high-maintenance
Enameled cast iron	Molten iron is poured into a mold and enamel coating is fired on	• Provides a warm, traditional look • More substantial than stainless steel • Available in many colors • Stays shiny for years • Quiet • Retains heat when filled with hot water • Materials less likely to chip than in the past	• More expensive than stainless or enameled steel • Very heavy so can be difficult to install	• Easy to clean • Low-maintenance

Material	Description	Advantages	Disadvantages	Care
Enameled steel	Steel stamped or pressed into shape, covered with an enamel finish, and then furnace-fired; the enamel layer is thinner than that on enameled cast iron	• Available in many colors • Resembles cast iron but is lighter and more flexible	• Thin and noisy • Doesn't stand up well to heavy use • Prone to chipping	• Easy to clean • Low-maintenance
Composite	Usually a speckled color and made of granite, quartz, or other materials mixed with acrylic or polyester-resin base	• Durable • Available in many colors • Nonporous and stain-resistant surfaces feature color throughout	• Expensive	• Easy to clean (avoid abrasive cleansers) • Low-maintenance
Fireclay	Clay base fired at intense heat to produce finish	• Durable, even more than enameled cast iron • Attractive glossy finish	• Limited variety of sizes and colors • Susceptible to chipping	• Low-maintenance
Vitreous china	Clay coated with a fired-on glaze	• Hard • Nonporous • Glasslike shine • Resists moisture and mildew • Resists discoloration and corrosion	• May chip if struck by a heavy object	• Easy to clean
Solid-surfacing	Polyester or acrylic base usually integrated with solid-surfacing countertop	• Available in countless colors • Resists scratches and chipping	• Specialized installation is required • Susceptible to burns	• Easy to clean • Used in integral sinks that have no joint or rim to trap dirt
Soapstone	Light gray stone with a smooth, soft texture that darkens with age	• Complements almost any design • Retains heat	• Costs more	• Easy to maintain
Slate	Natural stone with an organic look	• Complements almost any design • Retains heat	• Costs more	• Clean with warm, soapy water and rinse • Avoid abrasive cleansers or scrub pads
Granite	Natural stone that gives a textured look	• Complements many designs • Retains heat	• Costs more • Use restricted to hardest granite slabs that don't require sealing	• Clean with warm, soapy water and rinse • Avoid abrasive cleanser or scrub pads
Copper	With use, assumes warm, weathered patina	• Complements natural materials of country-style baths or metallic, contemporary setting • Finish may be hammered or smooth • Retains heat	• Expensive • Durable but is soft and can be dented or scratched	• Clean with mild dish detergent and soft cloth, then rinse with water and wipe dry with clean, soft cloth
Brass	Imparts warm metal look	• Complements traditional design • Retains heat	• Expensive • Durable but is soft and can be dented or scratched	• Clean with mild dish detergent and soft cloth, then rinse with water and wipe dry • Use professional brass cleaner to remove tarnish, then wipe with soft cloth

Sink, Tub, and Shower Fixtures

left and above Single-lever faucets offer smooth, clean looks or more adventuresome designs, as shown above. Fixtures are the jewels in a bathroom decorating scheme—choose them carefully.

If you're new to faucets, you will be impressed by the improved water-control mechanisms and replaceable cartridges or ceramic-disk valves as opposed to rubber washers. Washerless faucets are more expensive, but drips and leaks are essentially a problem of the past, so very few repairs are necessary. Also, most quality faucets are made of solid metal castings to which finishes are applied. Plastic castings are also available, but they are much less durable.

Large tubs require tub fillers (faucets) with high GPM (gallon per minute) fill rates to retain water heat while filling the tub.

Valve Options

There are four basic types of faucet valve mechanisms: ceramic-disk, cartridge, ball, and compression.

Ceramic-disk faucets have two ceramic disks that move against each other to block the flow of water. Generally more expensive, they're maintenance-free.

Cartridge-type faucets are available in single- and double-handle configurations and are designed for easy repair. The flow mechanisms are contained in a cartridge that is replaceable when a leak occurs.

Single-handle ball faucets have a rotating ball inside the faucet. The ball moves over water inlet holes, permitting water flow. It regulates the flow of hot and cold water and shuts off water.

Compression faucets with double handles have been around for about 100 years. A rubber washer stems the flow

of water. When the washer eventually becomes worn, the faucet tends to drip.

Installation Options

Installation options for faucets include single-hole, center-set, widespread, and wall-mount.

Single-hole models require just one hole on the sink ledge. They can have a single handle (usually connected to the spout) or hot- and cold-water handles.

Center-set faucets are one-piece fittings; the handles and spout are combined on a 4-inch base unit.

above Lever handles and cross handles are easy to grip. These handles control the tub spout on the other side of the tub as well as the handheld sprayer.

Widespread faucets separate the hot- and cold-water valves and the spout, giving more flexibility in placement. However, this model may cost twice as much as comparable center-set models.

Wall-mount faucets are mounted to the wall rather than the sink or countertop.

Mounting Options

Most sink faucets are installed directly onto the sink or countertop. Bathtub fixtures are installed on the tub, on the tub's platform, or on the wall. With undermount sinks, holes for the faucet are drilled directly into the countertop. With self-rimming sinks, the holes are in the sink. Make sure to match the number of holes you will need for your faucet with the number of holes drilled into the sink.

One Handle or Two?

You'll need to decide between one -or two-handle fixtures. Here are some key points to consider:

- A single-handle faucet allows you to control volume as well as hot and cold water temperatures with one hand.
- A single-handle faucet is ergonomically sound. For example, you can turn it on with a wrist or elbow if necessary.
- A single-handle faucet may require just one hole in the sink or tub ledge, making it easier to install.
- With one handle, spouts that swing have a greater swinging radius.
- Double-handle faucets offer a more traditional look. You also can independently control hot and cold temperatures with two handles.

Cost

- The least expensive faucet option is a basic two-handle, 4-inch center-set faucet in a chrome or lower-grade brass finish ($20 to $70).
- "Washerless" faucets with a variety of finish options and single or double handles are available in a wide variety of styles ($70 to $150 range).
- Higher-end styles include styled spouts; designer, decorative, and period pieces; and specialized finishes, such as no-tarnish brass or brushed nickel (up to $500).

Widespread faucet

Center-set faucet

Wall-mounted faucet

key ACCESSORIES

- An antiscald device limits the water temperature, eliminating the possibility of accidental scalding.
- A temporary-memory device attaches to a single-handle faucet and restricts the handle so that it can't reach the hottest setting.
- Hands-free operation/motion-sensor electronic faucets assist people with disabilities, arthritis sufferers, children, and anyone with wet hands.

Faucet Materials

Traditional chrome and brass finishes continue to be popular choices, but they have been joined by a wide selection ranging from muted metal tones to baked-on epoxy. Manufacturers have improved the way they apply finishes, leading to a wider choice of styles and materials that are durable and easy to clean. For example, some manufacturers are strengthening finishes with titanium to make them more wear-resistant. The finishes won't corrode or tarnish, and the colors won't fade.

When selecting a finish, some choose to match the fixture finish to the sink, countertop, or tub or shower fixtures. Personal preference may lead you to the traditional polished chrome or brass look, or you may lean toward the more muted finishes that blend well with stainless-steel elements. Many like the combination of matte faucet finishes with wood, stone, tile, and other popular materials being used for other elements. For general cost comparisons see page 117.

Material	Advantages	Disadvantages	Care
Chrome (polished, brushed, or matte finish)	• Chrome is common • Polished chrome is inexpensive, hard, and does not oxidize • Matte chrome has a softer appearance and is very durable	• Chrome over cheap plastic parts peels	• Easy to clean • Withstands abrasive cleaners
Colored (baked-on enamel or epoxy coating)	• Wide choice of deep, rich colors	• May chip • Can fade in sunlight, although epoxy finishes are tougher than enamel finishes • Prone to chemical change	• Easy to clean
Nickel (polished or brushed finish)	• Traditional appeal • Quality metal resists tarnish • Matte finish hides scratches	• Quality varies	• Clean with warm, soapy water
Brass (high-gloss, satin, or antique finish)	• Classic look • Fixtures with titanium finish resist scratching, fading, and corrosion	• Polished brass is prone to corrosion, scratching, and tarnishing	• Brass can tarnish unless a protective coating has been applied • Shine with rubbing alcohol
Copper (polished or brush finish)	• An old-fashioned look and simple beauty • Titanium-strengthened copper has a very durable finish	• Expensive • Quality varies • Requires finish by manufacturer or the copper may become damaged	• Clean with mild dish detergent and soft cloth, then rinse with water and wipe dry with a clean, soft cloth • Use professional copper cleaner to remove tarnish, then wipe with clean, soft cloth
Pewter (polished or brush finish)	• Visual appeal • Quality metal resists tarnish • Matte finish hides scratches	• Expensive • Quality varies	• Clean with warm, soapy water
Gold plate	• Visual appeal • Quality metal resists tarnish • Matte finish hides scratches	• Expensive • Quality varies • Requires finish by manufacturer or the gold may become damaged	• Clean with warm, soapy water

faucets FOR LIFE

PVD (physical, vapor, deposition) finishes on faucets today limit chips, scratches, pits, and tarnish. All major manufacturers offer a PVD finish with a lifetime warranty against product failure under normal use.

Bathtubs

If you have the space, consider separate tub and shower units. Fortunately, numerous modern tub/shower units are available, outfitted with features previously found only in luxury-level baths.

There are numerous shapes, sizes, and materials from which to choose. Just make sure the floor can support the tub of your choice.

Corner Tubs

This tub is not typically used where a tub/shower combination is desired. Available in 5- or 6-foot lengths, it's similar to a recessed tub. It uses more floor space than some other models. However, one type of corner tub fits diagonally in the corner, providing a more open feeling than a standard unit. You can outfit a corner tub with drains on either side or in the middle.

Freestanding Tubs

Claw-foot: It's built on four legs; all sides of the tub are visible.

Pedestal: Oval in shape, it does not rest on feet but rather on an oval base. Handheld showerheads are often added to pedestal tubs. One advantage over claw-foot: You don't have to clean under a pedestal tub.

sizing the TUB

Bathtubs are available in many shapes and sizes. Typical outside dimensions are 5 to 6 feet long. Remember that inside dimensions can vary in two tubs that have the same outside measurements. Climbing into a tub to try it out is probably the best way to get that perfect fit.

Recessed/Alcove Tubs

Reliable and typically having no frills, the alcove tub is still the most common tub type. It's enclosed on three sides and generally less expensive than a freestanding unit. This style is often used for tub/shower combinations. The faucets are typically wall-mounted. It's a good choice if you plan to install grab bars.

Drop-In or Platform Tubs

Floor-mounted sunken tubs are available, but they are very difficult to climb out of. That's why most drop-in tubs are mounted on a platform.

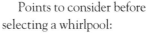

Whirlpool Tubs

A whirlpool tub gets its bubbling action from a water-circulating system with air mixed in. Most whirlpool baths have adjustable water jets that can target certain areas vigorously.

Points to consider before selecting a whirlpool:

- How much space do you have? Whirlpools start in 5- and 6-foot alcove configurations and get larger.
- What material will you use?
- How much weight can your floor hold?
- What is the water capacity of the tub you are considering, and what size water heater do you have?
- Do you want moveable and adjustable jets? How many? Placement?
- Do higher noise levels bother you?
- Can your wiring handle the electrical requirements?
- Do you want additional safety features, such as a mechanism in the water return that shuts the system off automatically if the return is blocked?
- Do you want a slip-resistant surface and grab bars?

Bathtub Materials

(For general cost comparisons see page 117.)

Material	Advantages	Disadvantages	Care
Plastic (either fiberglass or acrylic)	• Least expensive (can start at less than $100) • Can be molded into many shapes • High-gloss finish • Warm to the touch (keeps water warm longer than enameled-steel or cast-iron tub) • Lightest weight (60 to 70 pounds) • Does not chip or crack easily • Can be repaired if damaged • Acrylic tubs are more expensive than fiberglass but are more durable	• Can be damaged by abrasive cleaners • Less rigid, flexes with weight unless reinforced underneath	• Avoid abrasive cleaners
Enameled steel or porcelain on steel (formed steel with a heat-fused porcelain enamel coating)	• Inexpensive (typically $100–$300) • Relatively lightweight (between plastic and cast iron) • Resembles enameled cast iron • Smooth, attractive finish • Flameproof • Does not discolor or fade • Resistant to stains, corrosion, and abrasion	• Tub water cools quickly • Lower-priced models can be noisy when water is running into the tub • May be damaged by impact • Prone to chipping	• Easy to clean • Use nonabrasive cleaners
Cast iron (like steel, coated with enamel)	• More durable • Impact-resistant • Highly polished finish • More chip-resistant than enameled steel • Solid • Comes in a variety of colors • Retains heat fairly well • Quiet when water is running into the tub	• Very heavy (350 to 500 pounds) • Repairing or refinishing usually requires a professional	• Easy to clean • Low-maintenance
Cast polymer (made from solid-color polymer-based materials; resembles marble, granite, or onyx; and is finished with a polyester gel coat)	• Available in a range of solid colors • Holds heat well	• More expensive than acrylic • Not as durable as acrylic	• Avoid abrasive cleaners
Composite (heavy-gauge steel, porcelain enamel, and resins are combined)	• All the benefits of cast iron but weighs less • Not as noisy as cast iron • Retains heat	• Can be expensive	• Easy to clean (avoid abrasive cleaners) • Low-maintenance
Cultured marble (made from crushed limestone and polyester resin, with a gel-coated finish)	• Wide range of colors and patterns • Resists staining	• Can be scratched • Brittle • Must not fill with water that is too hot	• Easy to clean

faucet control valves = NO MORE OUCH

Two types of control valves alleviate abrupt changes in temperature: **pressure-balanced** and **thermostatic**.

■ Pressure-balanced valves monitor incoming hot and cold water and automatically adjust the combination to compensate for any changes in pressure.

■ Thermostatic valves monitor pressure and temperature, adjusting the flow of hot and cold water to maintain the temperature that is set by the user.

Showers

Showers offer comfort, convenience, and, increasingly, luxury. Shower units separate from the tub are recommended whenever space will permit. This offers the opportunity for two people to bathe at the same time, and separate showers are generally considered to be safer than tub/shower combinations in terms of ease of getting in and out of the shower.

Prefabricated Shower Stalls

Most prefabricated shower surrounds are made of fiberglass finished with acrylic or a polyester gel coat. They can also be made of vinyl, plastic laminate, or synthetic stone. One-piece units are attractive and functional, but they are so large they are best used in new construction. For remodeling projects, they can be very difficult, if not impossible, to get into the bathroom.

For most situations, you will be better off with a multipiece surround kit, which can be assembled inside the bathroom. Prefabricated stalls are designed to fit against a wall or in a corner. With most of these units, either shower curtains or shower doors can be used, and these are typically purchased separately. Prefabricated units are considered much easier to clean than custom stalls.

Many of the prefabricated stalls cannot accommodate some of the elaborate valves and fittings.

Prefabricated Shower Pans

Some prefabricated shower stalls come with a shower pan, or floor, while others require that a separate pan be installed. There are typically four standard pans from which to choose, including two sizes of rectangular, square, and neoangle.

Custom Stalls

Custom-made shower stalls naturally offer many options in terms of size, style, and materials, including beautiful tile and solid-surfacing. Some homeowners choose to fully seal

their shower stalls so that they can double as steam rooms. A growing trend is to include a large custom shower designed so that no door or curtain is needed. If you select a custom shower and you don't use a prefabricated shower pan, make sure you have a properly installed and sealed tile floor and drain.

Tub/Shower Combinations

Tub/shower combinations are a great space-saver and a versatile addition to a bath. With traditional construction, the walls around the tub are tiled with ceramic tile,

forming a shower enclosure. This continues to be a popular choice, but it does require maintenance, and leaks may develop over time. Another popular choice is a one-piece acrylic-over-fiberglass unit. Again, one-piece units may be difficult to get into the bathroom. These combinations are also available in sections.

Showerheads

Showerheads now include the traditional wall-mounted single showerheads, handheld showerheads, sliding-bar showerheads, massage heads, body-spray and body-mist showerheads, and deluxe overhead showerheads.

It's smart to consider an adjustable sliding bar with a removable handheld shower, either in combination with a fixed showerhead or by itself.

Handheld sprayers (whether with or without a sliding bar), which usually offer adjustable-flow settings, are becoming standard in tubs as well as in stand-alone shower units. The benefits are many, including the ease of rinsing hair and giving children a quick rinse after a bubble bath, and it also makes cleaning a tub or a shower much less a chore.

Overhead or pan-style showerheads, which provide the feeling of a waterfall or light rain shower, are typically used in combination with one or more additional showerheads. No matter what style showerhead you choose, you have a variety of choices in the type of spray, including conventional spray, aerated spray, massage spray, needle spray, soft-flow spray, and champagne spray.

Other Features

Body-spray showerheads are typically designed to have adjustable spray options and are mounted separately. They can be mounted at any height, and you can install as many as you wish. A "surround spray" effect can be achieved by mounting body-spray showers on opposite walls.

Body-mist showerheads emit a gentle spray and are typically designed as a series of jets on a bar. Make sure you set up your system so that you can choose whether to have the body-spray or body-mist units on or off at any given time. Depending on where they are mounted, you can also take a shower without getting your hair wet.

Body-spa showerheads are special panel units installed against the wall of the shower. These units have a series of vertical whirlpool-type jets from knee to neck level. These systems provide a powerful massage by pumping out and recirculating large quantities of water. The ultimate in shower luxury can be achieved by adding a steam unit, which is expensive but may get more use than a whirlpool.

Toilets and Bidets

Basic Shapes

- Standard toilets have round bowls and are 14 inches high. Models up to 17 inches high are available and are more comfortable for some users.
- Toilets and bidets with elongated bowls are more comfortable, but they are also more expensive.

Toilet Extras to Consider

- Electrically heated toilet seats
- Hydraulically operated seats
- Soft-closing seat systems that prevent the toilet seat from clanging down onto the toilet
- Personal-hygiene systems as an alternative to a bidet
- Hidden exhaust systems

Types of Bidet Valves

- Deck-mounted horizontal-spray bidet faucets are installed on the back of the bidet and are similar in design to standard sink faucets.
- Single- and double-control bidet faucets are available.
- With vertical-spray bidet valves, water from the valve is sprayed from a sprinkler located in the bowl of the fixture. These valves have a vacuum breaker that is designed to prevent contaminated water from re-entering the fresh water supply. They can be mounted on the back of the bidet or on the wall.

Toilets and bidets are usually sold in pairs. Unless they will be installed in separate locations, it's wise to buy a matched set to maintain a cohesive design. Like toilets, bidets are available in round and elongated styles.

Bidets can be more difficult to install than toilets, primarily because they are not as standardized. Also, bidets require a valve to turn on and off the water.

While one-piece toilets provide a sleeker, more contemporary look and are easier to clean, two-piece toilets are the standard design. Wall-mounted toilets have a tank "hidden" in the wall and discharge to the rear rather than through the floor. These toilets are quieter and offer a very contemporary look.

Go with the Low-Flow

All toilets are required by law to be low-flow models. There are three types of low-flow toilets:

- **Gravity-flush toilets:** The weight of the water flowing down from the tank clears the bowl. These are usually the least expensive, but they are not as effective as the other types.
- **Pressure-assisted toilets:** In these toilets, pressurized air in the pressure vessel forces water into the bowl and then down the drain. These toilets are more expensive and are noisy, but they are the most effective.
- **Pump-assisted toilets:** A pump below the tank propels water into the bowl and then down the drain. These are expensive. They tend to match the effectiveness of pressure-assisted but are much quieter.

above Anatomy of a gravity-flush toilet. Advances in design have provided increased pressure to assist in removing waste.

Cabinets

Bathroom cabinetry can vary from small vanities to large furniture-like units. Material and accessory choices are numerous, but before browsing, first review the basics of how cabinets are built (framed and frameless); the three categories of cabinets or vanities (stock, built-to-order or semicustom, and custom); tips about doors, drawers, and hardware; and information about must-have accessories. Cabinet hardware does not come with the cabinets and holes are not predrilled; you will select the appropriate knobs and pulls after you have chosen the cabinets.

Cabinet Types

Cabinets fall into three basic categories, depending on how they're constructed and whether they can be customized. They are stock, built-to-order, or custom-made. There are two basic styles of construction—framed and frameless (see page 136).

Stock Cabinets
- Sold fully assembled or ready to assemble (RTA).
- They're available in a standard range of styles and sizes.
- Most are sold fully assembled.
- They are typically constructed of particleboard, with doors, drawers, and face frames made of hardwood.
- Stock units are made in 3-inch-wide increments (the smallest is 9 inches wide and the largest 48 inches).
- Typically, those less than 24 inches wide have one door, and wider cabinets are designed with two doors.
- The quality can be excellent, but materials and accessory options may be limited.

Built-to-Order (Semi-custom)
- These cabinets are midrange in terms of both cost and options.
- They are built by a manufacturer according to a limited range of specifications, with more design flexibility than stock cabinets (more choices in cabinet sizes; certain types of interior fittings, such as pullout shelves and lazy Susans; and a variety of door styles, hardware, and finishes).
- Materials tend to be a higher grade than those used in stock units and include medium-density fiberboard (MDF), which is superior to particleboard, better-quality wood laminates, and durable varnishes.
- You may wait from 3 to 12 weeks for delivery, depending on the complexity of the job.

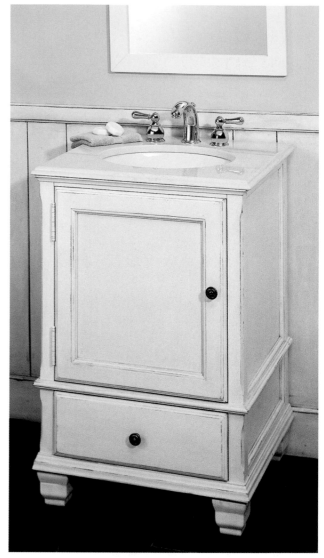

above The cabinet style used to construct this vanity is called framed because the hinges are fixed to the rails of the cabinet.

Custom
- These cabinets are usually the most expensive option.
- They are built to suit specific needs, with the work done by local cabinetmakers, though some factory-made lines will allow you to order a custom bathroom. It's possible to order custom cabinets through bathroom dealers and home centers.
- If you want to keep some of your existing units, a custom cabinetmaker can produce new ones to match.
- If you need to solve an unusual layout problem that can't be solved with stock or semicustom products, custom cabinets offer an answer.
- You can select the material of your choice: solid wood or plywood, MDF, or particleboard covered with laminate or wood veneer.

Standard Cabinet Dimensions

Wall Cabinets

Wall cabinets, which are units that are attached to or mounted in the wall, are not as common in a bath as in a kitchen, but in larger baths, where space permits, they are a welcome feature, offering additional storage and design impact. A common type of wall cabinet is the small cabinet often found over the toilet. Another popular choice is a floor-to-ceiling cabinet/storage unit, similar to units often found in kitchens, or a narrower specialty linen cabinet.

left A floor-to-ceiling wall cabinet offers both storage and display.

right Primary storage in a bathroom comes in the form of base cabinets, which have a wide variety of options, including doors, drawers, and slide-out trays.

Bathroom Cabinets

Bathroom cabinets include sink base units and a variety of specialty units including linen towers and wall units.

- The height of available base units ranges from 29 to 34½ inches (this height includes the toe-kick, which is the 3-inch recess along the bottom front of the cabinet).
- The standard depth is 18 or 21 inches.
- The width is anywhere from 12 to 48 inches, in 3-inch increments (units with a single drawer over a door typically vary in width from 12 to 24 inches, while units with double doors and a single shelf typically range in width from 27 to 48 inches).
- Base units can have doors, drawers, or a combination of the two.
- Most cabinet manufacturers offer base units with a variety of accessories, such as slide-out hampers for storage.
- Sink units are typically 18 to 48 inches wide with two doors and false drawer fronts.

left Providing a combination of drawers and doors keeps the lines of the bathroom clean while providing a place for toiletries and supplies.

Framed or Frameless

Framed Cabinets

Framed cabinets have been around for centuries and are more traditional. The exposed edges of the frame (the reveal) are visible around the doors and drawers.

- This cabinet has the most traditional look and type of construction.
- The face frame is attached to the front of the cabinet box.
- The frame is purposely made to be slightly wider than the cabinets. When two cabinets are placed together, the frames automatically form a tight seam.
- The frame reinforces the box, and the doors are hung from it with exterior hinges that are attached to both the face frame and the inside face of the door.
- The hinges attaching the doors to the frame may be either exposed or hidden.
- The cabinet sides fit into the face-frame stile and are glued, nailed, or stapled into place.
- The cabinet typically includes removable shelves that rest on adjustable brackets.
- Stock framed cabinets can come as wide as 48 inches (custom cabinets can be even wider).
- The frame and vertical stiles between doors make the box opening smaller.
- The drawer box fronts are often covered with false panels, which are screwed to the drawer front, are usually larger than the drawer front, and overlay the face frame around the drawer opening.

Frameless Cabinets

Compared to framed cabinets, this cabinet type is a more recent development, offering a more contemporary look.

- There is no face frame; rather, a hinge supports a door nearly as wide as the cabinet.
- Access is easier, with slightly more space inside.
- Shelves are usually adjustable.
- A roll-out shelf can take up the entire width of the cabinet.
- Until installed, frameless cabinets are less rigid than framed; after installation, they are extremely solid and are supported by one another and the bathroom wall. (If squaring them up yourself during installation, take your time.)
- A design that uses a frameless cabinet may need to allow for additional door clearance.
- Frameless cabinets most commonly have been made of laminate, but wood is increasingly available.

> ## inspect the
> ## CABINETS
>
> Inspect your cabinets for damage **on delivery!** Don't wait until the installer arrives to open the boxes. Damaged cabinets guarantee delays while waiting for replacements

Cabinet Anatomy

Understanding the different cabinet parts will help you make the best selection. After reviewing this information, start browsing and take your time.

Here are the types of substrates used in most cabinets:

Cabinet Substrates

Particleboard:

- This substrate is made of wood particles mixed with resin and bonded under pressure.
- Cabinet interiors are often made of particleboard, particularly cabinetry that will be covered with laminate and vinyl film.
- Advances in manufacturing have improved its strength and reliability, but watch out for poor grades.

Medium-Density Fiberboard (MDF):

- This high-quality material is made from fibers finer than those used in particleboard.
- The surface is much smoother.
- The edges can be shaped and painted.
- This substrate offers superior screw-holding power.

Plywood/Engineered Wood:

- These substrates are made by laminating thin layers of wood plies onto each other.
- The grain of one layer is run at a right angle to the grain of the previous layer, giving plywood equal strength in all directions.
- The layers are bonded with glue under heat and pressure.
- Thin plywood is often used for cabinet backs; thicker plywood is used for cabinet sides.

Cabinet Surface Materials

The materials used as cabinet finishes fall into two primary categories: laminates and wood veneers. A laminate surface is made of three resin-saturated layers (a base layer of paper, a printed and colored layer, and a protective transparent layer). Heat and pressure fuse the laminate to the substrate. Choices in color, pattern, and quality vary widely. Here is an overview of common laminate options:

- **High-pressure laminates** provide vertical surfaces with the same durability as countertops, but they are more expensive.
- **Low-pressure laminates,** also called melamine, are less impact-resistant than high-pressure laminates and have a tendency to crack and chip, but use of better substrates can reduce these problems.
- **Resin-impregnated foils** and heat-stamped transfer foils come in wood grains and some solid colors. The heavier the weight, the better the scuff resistance. These

frame of REFERENCE

As you inspect cabinets and talk over decisions with professionals, you'll want to know basic construction terms.

- **Biscuit joint:** a joint held together by thin wooden ovals which are embedded between the two pieces to be seamed with a special joiner. Commonly used to hold postform laminate countertops together.
- **Center stile:** the middle strut in a framed cabinet (also called a mullion).
- **Cross member:** a horizontal support in a frameless cabinet.
- **Dado joint:** a joint between two pieces of wood where one piece fits into a notch, or dado, cut in a second piece.
- **Dovetail joint:** an interlocking corner joint where pins on one piece fit into sockets on a second piece.
- **Dowel pegged joint:** a joint held together with dowel pins.
- **Filler:** a strip of wood placed between cabinets at corners to ensure doors and drawers open freely; it also fills gaps between the cabinet and the wall or helps set the cabinet plumb and level.
- **Intarsia:** a decorative groove cut into the top and bottom of cabinets; the top groove can replace a doorknob or handle.
- **Rabbet:** a wood joint in which one piece fits into a groove cut along the edge of the other piece.
- **Rail:** a horizontal crosspiece in a cabinet face frame or door (a rail at least ¾ inch thick helps solidify cabinets).
- **Reveal:** on a framed cabinet, the distance between the edge of the face frame and the edge of the door, usually ³⁄₁₆ to ¼ inch.
- **Shim:** a thin, wedge-shaped piece of wood used to fill gaps between a cabinet and the wall to level the unit.
- **Stile:** a vertical piece of cabinet face frame or door.

laminates generally are applied to cover curves and contours. The seams are undetectable.

- **Thermofoil** is a vinyl film applied to a substrate with heat and pressure. It resembles wood more closely than other laminates. It's easy to care for and less likely to chip than painted cabinets.

Types of Cabinet Wood

Hard Maple
- Popular in semicustom or custom cabinetry
- Fine, straight grain and light color
- Stable and durable
- Slightly more expensive than oak

Red Oak
- Used in stock or semicustom cabinetry
- Often used to create a traditional look
- Strong, durable, and relatively inexpensive
- Pronounced grain patterns, open grain

Birch
- Used in stock or semicustom cabinetry
- Slightly darker than maple
- Can be stained to achieve the look of cherry or maple
- Durable or fine-grain wood

Cherry
- Used in stock or semicustom cabinetry
- Stands up well to heavy use
- Darkens with age, so is usually stained to ensure uniformity of color
- Used in traditional and contemporary styles

Pine
- Usually used in semicustom cabinets
- The only soft wood recommended for cabinets, but dents easily
- Can be stained
- Used in traditional and country styles

Ash
- Used in custom and some semicustom cabinets
- Similar to oak in strength and durability
- Lighter than oak
- Often used in contemporary styles

Hickory
- Used in custom or semicustom cabinets
- Lighter in color than oak
- Can be stained but works best with clear or natural finish
- Best with rustic styles

White Oak
- Generally used only in custom cabinets
- Slightly stronger than red oak
- Durable

The Core of the Cabinet: The Box and the Drawers

Spend plenty of time looking at cabinets in showrooms. Soon you'll develop an eye for quality by visiting showrooms and home centers. Take your time looking. Here are some points to keep in mind:

- The best wood cabinets have solid doors with the grain running in the same direction on exposed sides, backs, drawer fronts, doors, and shelves.
- Drawers are made of solid wood or plywood.
- The side panel, back panel, and floorboard of a cabinet are typically made of plywood, particleboard, or MDF that has been covered with veneer.
- Less expensive cabinets have doors and frames made of plywood, veneered particleboard, or wood-grain laminate.
- Regardless of material, the door and drawer edges should be smooth to the touch.

- The best joint for a cabinet box is a dado joint, in which the sides fit into grooves that have been cut into the cabinet back and the face frame. Dado joints are more stable than those that have been butted and glued.
- Corner gussets—triangular braces glued into the upper corners of the cabinet box—add strength.
- The back panel adds strength and guards against invasion by insects and vermin.
- Plastic clips hold false drawer fronts in place.
- Many wood cabinets will arrive on site with a finish applied by the factory or cabinetmaker. If they are unfinished, finish them as soon as they are installed to prevent warping. Cabinet doors are particularly vulnerable.

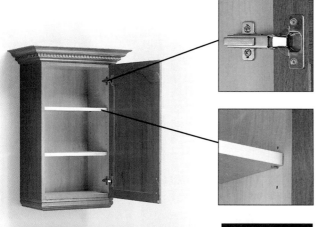

Adjustable metal hinges help align doors on frameless cabinets.

A close look at individual components will reveal much about the quality of bathroom cabinets. Adjustable shelves are usually held in place with easily movable pins or clips.

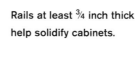

Rails at least ¾ inch thick help solidify cabinets.

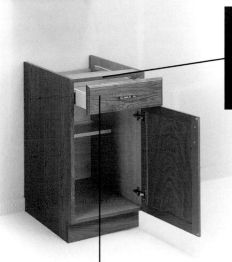

Well-constructed drawers are the best indication of fine quality: Look for interlocking joinery, thick bottoms, and smooth-running slides.

Cabinet Shelves

- Look for shelves that are made from ¾-inch high-grade particleboard that has been covered with veneer.
- Adjustable shelves are usually held in place with easily movable pins or clips that have been inserted into holes drilled along the inside of the cabinet box.
- Many cabinets now come equipped with roll-out trays, which are a cross between a drawer and a shelf. These should be installed with the same high-quality slides recommended for drawers.

Door Styles

The look of cabinet doors makes a strong first impression, contributing to the overall bathroom design. Although many varieties exist, they fall into two primary categories: slab and frame-and-panel.

Slab Doors

- Clean lines offer a more contemporary look.
- Slab doors are typically made of several pieces of wood glued together, giving the appearance of a single panel of wood.
- These doors are most often used in the full-overlay style.

Frame-and-Panel Doors

- The panels are set in grooves inside the frame, giving the wood room to swell or shrink with changes in humidity. If the panels were glued to the frame, the door might crack or warp.
- In a combination door, the frame consists of lumber, and the panel is of plywood.
- If the panel is flat, the door is referred to as a recessed-panel door.
- If the center of the panel is raised, the door is referred to as a raised-panel door.
- If glass, metal, or another type of insert is used rather than a wood panel, it is secured against an open lip on the back, not within the frame.

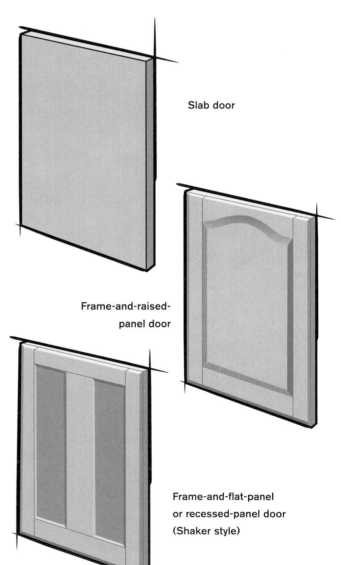

Slab door

Frame-and-raised-panel door

Frame-and-flat-panel or recessed-panel door (Shaker style)

---

selecting
WOOD VENEER

Wood veneer comes from peeling strips of wood off a tree. Thinner than solid wood, it's adhered to plywood or particleboard. Available on higher-end cabinets, wood veneer gives them warmth and texture. When selecting a wood veneer, assess the grain, density, and color, but remember that wood can be treated with a variety of stains to achieve different looks. For example, a stain can replicate the look of maple on a birch base.

How Doors Fit

Now that you have an idea of the cabinet type that you want to grace your bathroom, here are different types of cabinet doors that are available. How a door fits over the cabinet box determines its basic classification.

Partial Overlay
- The door is large enough to cover the opening but small enough to reveal the cabinet's frame.
- It is the least expensive and easiest to construct.

Full Overlay
- The door covers the face frame (or the entire box front on frameless cabinets).
- Only a sliver of space exists between doors and drawers.
- Only full overlay is used on frameless cabinets.

Flush-Inset
- The doors and drawers fit flush with the face frame.
- A precision fit is available only in custom cabinets.

Lipped
- To fit over the face frame, the door is routed with a wooden groove.

above A framed vanity cabinet with partial overlay doors offers a traditional look.

Framed

Frame up. In framed cabinets, doors may be flush with the front face of the frame or overlay it. In partial overlays the edges of the door reveal part of the frame. In full overlay doors, the doors sit on the front stiles of the cabinets.

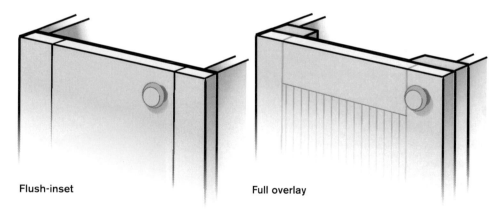

Flush-inset

Full overlay

Frameless

Clean lines. On frameless cabinets, recessed doors sit flush with the front edge of the cabinet sides. Full-overlay doors sit on the front of the cabinets. These options are available in framed cabinets as well.

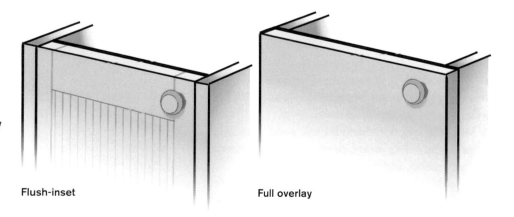

Flush-inset

Full overlay

Drawers

You can easily determine overall quality by examining drawer construction. Also test the drawers. Check how smoothly the drawer moves in and out, and make sure you can easily access the interior.

Drawer Fronts

The visible part of the drawer is constructed two ways.

■ An inset, or flush-front, drawer closes so that its face is flush with the surrounding cabinet.

■ The overlay drawer has a false front screwed to the drawer. It extends past the edges and top of the drawer front.

Solid Drawer Bottom

■ Look for ½- or ¾-inch solid wood sides and a plywood bottom panel at least ³⁄₁₆ to ¼ inch thick that has been glued into grooves.

■ Thinner bottoms (⅛ inch thick) may buckle under the weight of heavy loads.

■ Make sure bottoms are set in the routed grooves of all four sides.

■ Solid wood bottoms may "float" to accommodate expansion and contraction due to changes in humidity, but plywood bottoms are often glued.

Quiet, Smooth Slides

■ Quality slides are rated to support at least 75 pounds.

■ You should be able to pull out a drawer easily and silently whether opening it partially or all the way.

■ Full-extension slides, which attach to the bottom or sides of the drawer and have a ball-bearing system, allow full access to the inside of the drawer. Make sure they have stops so that they don't roll completely out of the cabinet. Although more expensive, they offer stability.

■ Solid-metal slides with ball bearings have bumpers to cushion the impact of the drawer as it closes. Their runners mount to the bottom of the drawer.

■ Nylon rollers on steel tracks attach to the sides of drawers. They're quiet but not as reliable as slides with ball bearings.

■ When a drawer is opened an inch, it should close on its own.

■ Side-mount slides are more common, but drawers with a bottom-mount mechanism save space on both sides and offer a higher-quality look.

■ Other slides have releases so that you can remove them from cabinets for cleaning.

Cabinet Hardware

Knobs and Pulls

Cabinet hardware should be functional, but it should also impact the overall style. Knobs and pulls of all shapes and sizes are available in home centers, hardware stores, and even department stores. Shop catalogs and online, as well as flea markets and antiques stores.

■ Materials selections include glass, wood, resin, ceramic, metal (including nickel, pewter, chrome, bronze, and iron), rubber, and stone.

■ Styles are almost endless: reproductions from certain periods, whimsical shapes reflecting special interests or hobbies, and shapes to complement the cabinet styles and other decorative features of the bathroom.

■ Knobs should be comfortable to grasp, sturdy, and easy to use.

Hinges

■ Hinges can be entirely visible, partially visible, or hidden.

■ With visible hinges, choose a style that blends in with the other cabinet hardware.

■ Invisible hinges fit both framed and frameless cabinets, allow for several opening and closing options, and are fully adjustable.

Storage Options

You'll want to use every inch of storage space in your bathroom cabinets. The number and variety of accessories are astounding. Make planning storage part of your remodeling plan. Home centers are sources of good advice about efficient storage. Consider accessories that not only keep your bathroom organized but also minimize stooping, bending over, and reaching.

Open shelving

Divided storage in drawers

Open linen storage

Built-in or pull-out laundry hamper

Storage space recessed in wall

Decorative linen and toiletries storage

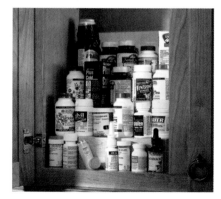

Stacked medicine storage

More Storage Options

- Double- or-single-sink vanity base cabinets
- Furniture-style vanities
- Built-in makeup area with lower countertop allowing for seated grooming
- Medicine cabinets
- Drawers with storage dividers
- Linen closet
- Open shelving (great for towels, soaps, and decorative items)
- Tall, narrow cabinet near toilet for scrub brushes and cleaners
- Built-in niche in closet for laundry baskets
- Enclosed storage for kids' needs (supplies and toys)

- Fold-down shelf/door that serves as a step stool for children
- Rolling/mobile shelves or storage unit
- Towel bars, hooks, and racks (various finishes, including brass, hammered and unhammered copper, satin nickel, regal gold, and pewter)
- Heated towel racks or bars
- Towel-warming drawer
- Hand towel rings
- Freestanding furniture
- Revolving trays in cabinets
- Built-in ironing board

Countertops

Along with the floor, countertops are one of the hardest-working surfaces in the bathroom. They are also important design elements because of their high visibility. Many of today's bathrooms mix and match countertop materials. This can create a distinctive look and lets you incorporate surfaces that are best suited to their specific function. Special edge treatments offer interesting detail. Edges can be an integral part of the countertop or can be added molded pieces. Solid-surfacing countertops, for example, can be worked just like wood to create a variety of edging shapes.

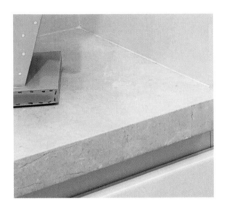

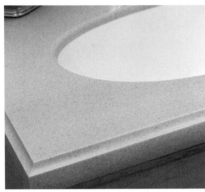

Laminate

Counters are made of thin layers of plastic bonded to a core of particleboard. Color-through laminate is available, which has color throughout the thickness of the sheet. This is more expensive but offers a better look. With custom or special-order laminate, the edge of the counter is built up; a variety of edge treatments is available.

Solid-Surfacing

These countertops are made from polyester or acrylic resins or a combination of both. A one-piece integrated countertop and sink is popular with solid-surfacing.

Ceramic Tile

You can use either floor or wall tiles for countertops. For countertops that will see heavy use, the more durable floor tiles are recommended.

(For general cost comparisons see page 117.)

Material	Advantages	Disadvantages	Care
Laminate (prefab, special-order)	• Durable • Stain resistant • Wide variety of colors and finishes • Easy to install • Moderate price	• Glossy finishes may look great when new but tend to show dirt and scratches over time • Cannot be repaired if damaged, burned, or stained	• Low maintenance
Solid-surfacing	• Very durable • Customization available • Available in many colors, patterns, and finishes • Can mimic granite and other stones • Solid color throughout • Some damage can be sanded away	• Although some DIY installations are possible, custom installations must be done by profesionals to ensure warranty coverage • Scratchable surface • High-gloss finish on a dark counter can show scratches and nicks	• Easy to clean • Shallow cuts can be sanded out with an abrasive pad
Ceramic tile (stock, custom, patterned, and hand-painted)	• Durable • Available in many shapes, sizes, patterns, and colors • Stock tiles comparable in price to laminate • Moisture-resistant	• Slightly uneven surface due to grout lines • Difficult to remove	• Glazed tiles easy to clean • Grout line easily stained and difficult to keep clean

  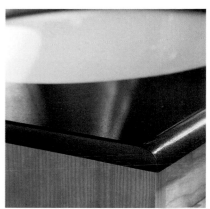

Stone Tile and Slabs

Marble, limestone, slate, soapstone, lava stone, sandstone, and granite or marble tiles are all available for countertops. Stone adds elegance to a bathroom space. Slab granite (**above left**) is durable and lends itself to both contemporary and traditional looks. Limestone (**above right**) has the durability of granite but comes in softer, more muted colors.

(For general cost comparisons see page 117.)

Quartz Surfacing

A stone surface made of 93 percent natural quartz along with binders and pigments to create more consistent color and higher performance than other natural stones.

Material	Advantages	Disadvantages	Care
Stone tile and slabs	• Extremely durable • Granite or marble tiles less expensive and easier to handle than slabs of stone • Granite less porous than marble and stain- and scratch-resistant	• Can be expensive • Heavy and difficult to install • Some marble stains easily	• Dark, glossy colors of granite can be difficult to clean • Marble should be resealed frequently • Granite and marble should be sealed and polished on a regular basis
Butcher block or hardwood	• Warm and beautiful • Some damage can be smoothed out with sandpaper	• Can be damaged by water	• High-maintenance • Finishing oil should be applied frequently
Stainless steel	• Durable • Does not stain • Great professional and contemporary look	• More difficult to install • Scratches easily • Some find it noisy	• Easy to clean
Cast concrete	• Durable • Can be finished to be smooth or textured • Available in many colors	• Expensive	• When sealed, the surface is easy to clean
Soapstone	• Elegant texture and color	• Soft and prone to scratches	• Should be sealed periodically with mineral oil
Quartz surfacing	• High performance • Consistent color • Variety of colors available • Durable	• Installation can be time intensive	• Easy to clean with soap and water • Resists stains

countertop TIMING

Solid-surfacing, quartz surfacing, and natural stone countertops require that a full-size template be made on site before fabrication to guarantee a good fit. You must add the appropriate time to the installation process and assume that you will be using temporary tops for a few weeks until the top is finished.

Lighting

With artificial lighting, your design should achieve the best mix of ambient, task, and accent lighting, ensuring sufficient general and task lighting in every functional area.

Ambient Lighting

Ambient lighting is the general lighting that fills the room. During the day, sunlight can provide much of the bathroom's ambient lighting. You also should install adequate ceiling fixtures, track lighting, and/or recessed fixtures. Lighting from ceiling fixtures alone can create unpleasant shadows.

How much light is enough? With ambient lighting, for each 50 square feet of floor space, you should have at least 100 watts of incandescent light or 75 watts of fluorescent light. You need to consider the height of your ceiling and the color of your walls. Darker colors tend to absorb light, so if your decorating scheme relies on darker tones, you may need additional lighting.

Task Lighting

Task lighting provides direct light in areas such as above vanities and in the shower and for the tub. Many types of fixtures, including recessed downlights, track lights, hanging pendent lights, and undercabinet strip lights, provide excellent task lighting. It's best to control the lighting for each work center with a separate wall switch.

How much task light do you need? Each task area should be illuminated with at least either 100 to 150 watts of incandescent light or 40 to 50 watts of fluorescent light.

Accent Lighting

Accent lighting increases the design impact of your bathroom area and is typically about three times more powerful than general lighting. Accent lights are used to create focus on specific areas or objects in a bathroom such as fixtures, display shelving, or an interesting architectural feature or element. Fixed accent lights are usually halogen bulbs that point a highly focused beam of bright light in a particular direction and are usually placed in recessed fixtures or mounted on a ceiling track or wall. An accent light can also be a table or floor lamp carefully placed to highlight a specific area.

bulb BLURBS

- Incandescent lights generate a warm glow. They enhance yellow and red hues and are flattering to skin tones, are inexpensive, are easy to change, and come in many styles.
- Fluorescent lights last up to 20 times longer and generate up to four times more light than same-wattage incandescent bulbs. Some fluorescent bulbs give off a much warmer, softer glow than was available in the past. Some types of fluorescents can be dimmed.

- Halogen lights last twice as long as incandescent bulbs and are up to three times brighter. Halogen lights radiate all the colors of the spectrum so that the light they produce reflects decorative elements in their true colors. Halogen lights are small and can be installed in unobtrusive fixtures, such as those popular for undercabinet lighting. These bulbs are more expensive than either incandescent or fluorescent, they burn at higher temperatures, they are more fragile, and they can be damaged if they come into contact with oily substances.

Flooring

A bathroom floor must withstand water, heat, moisture, and humidity, and most important, be slip-resistant.

Resilient

Resilient flooring describes all synthetic, resin-based flooring and includes vinyl tiles, sheet flooring, linoleum, cork, and rubber. Although comfortable, resilient flooring dents easily.

Vinyl, the most common type of resilient flooring, is inexpensive, flexible, and available in many colors and designs. Some vinyl floors mimic stone and ceramic tile. Vinyl resists water and stains and is relatively soft.

You can purchase vinyl in sheets or tiles. Vinyl tiles are easier to install for homeowners and less expensive. Sheet vinyl is slightly more expensive than the tiles but is seamless which makes for easier cleaning.

Linoleum is durable and actually becomes harder the longer it is down. Linoleum costs about twice as much as quality vinyl sheet flooring, but it is still significantly less expensive than hardwood flooring.

Other choices include **cork** and **rubber,** which are available in muted shades.

Laminate

Laminate flooring comes in planks (which mimic materials such as stone and wood) and tiles (which can also resemble real tiles or stone). It is stronger and more durable than laminate countertops. This type of flooring resists stains, warping, and scratching, and it is very easy to clean.

Wood

Hardwood, a very durable and fairly forgiving surface, is available in a vast array of shades and grain patterns. Most of today's wood floor finishes are suitable for bathrooms.

The most durable hardwoods are oak, maple, and cherry. Softwoods, such as pine, will dent. However, a distressed pine floor suits a country style. Hardwood requires occasional refinishing to remove scratches and marred areas. Wipe up spills immediately.

Ceramic and Stone

Ceramic tile looks great and is easy to clean. This type of flooring has design versatility, as it is available in a myriad of shapes, sizes, textures, and colors. Pattern possibilities are limitless.

Stone tiles (marble, limestone, slate, granite) offer a beautiful, natural look. Most natural stone tiles come in pieces that are 12 inches square and 3 to 8 inches thick. Most professionals choose to use thin grout lines and match the grout color to the color of the stone tiles. Some stones stain easily, and some are not strong enough to be used for flooring, so be careful when making your selection.

Stone is often heavier than other surfaces. The subfloor often needs to be reinforced to support the weight of the stone. Granite and limestone should be sealed periodically. A low-sheen wax or acrylic sealer can be applied to slate.

Fine Details

Give your bath personality with attention to detail. Express your style by accentuating the ceiling, windows, and walls.

You may think of finishing touches as enhancements that are added once your remodeling project or addition is finished. After all your hard work, it's fun to choose paint colors, window treatments, and plants. Be aware, however, that you need to plan certain details long before the completion date. Architectural elements such as ceilings, columns, and windows need to be decided in advance.

Decorative accents offer an opportunity to reinforce style. For inspiration, review the elements of style in Chapter 1. Also flip through magazine clippings stored in your brainstorm book for decorating ideas that will give your bath character. Browse the aisles of home centers, accessory stores, and walk through designer show houses for additional inspiration.

CHAPTER 5 CONTENTS

left Carefully chosen accessories and accents complete your bathroom design. Towel rings and racks, soap dishes, storage units, flower vases, accessories on trays, and plumbing fixtures are some of the finishing touches that provide both functionality and appeal.

Ceiling Accents

The beauty of a room does not just surround you. It can cause your gaze to sweep upward. Why roll just a coat of paint on your ceiling? Instead, make it a focal point by varying textures and materials to create dynamic shapes and lines. Add accent windows or recessed lighting for ambience and detail.

top right Varying the planes in a ceiling creates changing shape and line depending on the time of day and the use of ambient light.

right Combining wallpaper and a tongue-and-groove wooden ceiling provides both rhythm and texture.

far right Accent windows offer visual interest and allow natural light to play on the planes of walls and ceilings.

Sinks Are Details Too

Bathroom sinks come in so many shapes, materials, colors, and styles that it's easy to match and amplify any decorating scheme. Often bathrooms are built around a particular style of sink. Research all the options as you're planning and designing your bathroom, and don't settle until you've found exactly what you want.

top right Graceful lines and smooth curves recreate a traditional 1930s look for the basin of this pedestal sink.

right Natural stone provides both color and texture for this countertop with an undermounted sink.

right Pictures and nursery rhymes on this fanciful sink are perfect for a children's bath.

Functional Display

Towels, soap, and toiletries may be primarily functional items, but they also have strong design appeal. Take full advantage of the possibilities by artfully displaying them on towel racks, open shelving, built-in niches, or in baskets by the bath or shower.

right A family photograph, a shaving brush, and clear canisters filled with toiletries work easily together.

left A woven basket holds soap and towels.

far left Contemporary open shelving is useful and decorative.

Take Your Medicine

You can have more than just a mirror above the vanity. Medicine chests with hidden shelving serve several purposes, all of which are equally important in a successful bathroom plan. Medicine chests store frequently used supplies and keep them out of sight. Mirrors and good lighting make morning and evening rituals, such as shaving or applying makeup, easier to manage. And they act as prominent and defining design elements in the overall decorating scheme.

right A toiletries cabinet mounted in the sidewall of a vanity area matches the rest of the bathroom's woodwork.

far right Stairstep shelving in medicine cabinets help organize bottles making everything easier to find.

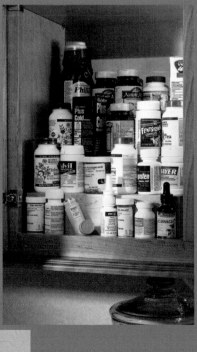

Storage, Storage, Storage

Any design is most effective when the room is uncluttered and provides a sense of order. Linen and storage closets in a bathroom keep towels and supplies available but hidden so you can display only those elements that add definition and focus to your bathroom. The closet doors also add architectural detail to the space. Built-in storage in or near a bathroom area can also serve as organized closet space for clothing and shoes.

above and left Large enclosed linen storage keeps towels in order.

far left Built-in cabinetry in dressing areas near the master bath provides easy and organized access.

below and center Natural stone tiles offer variety in both color and texture, plus they are easy to maintain.

below right Strip hardwood flooring complements wooden cabinetry. It works well in dressing areas.

More Than Just a Floor

The floor is sometimes referred to as the fifth wall because you must pay as much attention to what covers it as you would for the walls themselves. The right flooring provides comfort and safety, functions as a unifying design element, and creates successful transitions between rooms. Consider mixing textures and colors to create unique patterns and combinations.

Lighting Is a Key

Lighting is a major factor in creating a relaxing and comforting ambience in a bathroom. As with most of the elements that make up a bathroom, lighting serves both a practical and aesthetic function. As a design element, lighting, whether natural or ambient, creates mood and focus. Proper lighting is also essential for safety and for making the bathroom efficient and easy to use.

above A three-light fixture provides good illumination above a vanity mirror.

left Wall sconces offer ambient light and decorative accents.

far left Sheer curtains allow natural light and a little privacy.

Go With the Flow

Faucets are considered the jewels of the bathroom. They are available in literally hundreds of models, configurations, and materials to suit any design requirement. If you've got to wash your hands anyway, you might as well do it in style.

left and right Contemporary designs and finishes are clean and simple in design. Innovations in spout design produce interesting patterns of water flow.

below left and right Traditionally designed faucet fixtures are both elegant and luxurious. Bright brass finishes add color to any bathroom.

Universal Design

Universal design makes this bathroom convenient and comfortable for everyone without sacrificing style.

The beauty of universal design is its ability to accommodate all people through all of life's stages and changes. If you're in the early planning stages of building or renovating a bath, incorporating universal design is a wise investment.

No matter what circumstances arise—a family member becoming permanently or temporarily disabled, a young child or a shorter-than-average adult needing assistance, or a friend with a disability dropping by for a visit—you won't need to make significant changes to a universally built bath. Free of obstacles, your bathroom becomes usable by all. And if you're planning to live in your home for many years, universal design features will eventually accommodate your own changing needs. Successful implementation of this approach features virtually invisible results in an attractive, functional bathroom.

CHAPTER 6 CONTENTS

left This bathroom anticipates the needs of the owners should an older parent with reduced strength or stamina come to live with them or should the homeowners need assistance in their own later years. Structural reinforcing that accommodates grab bars is built into the walls.

Universal Design: Easy-Working Bathroom

With particular attention to placement, shape, and size, universal design features go practically undetected. For instance, if you put light switches and electrical outlets at heights accessible to your young daughter, most users will not notice the subtle change.

In the same vein, the shape of something as simple as a doorknob affects how easily a person enters and leaves a room but doesn't necessarily draw undue attention. Comparably priced lever-style door handles are easier to grasp than knobs and are available in a range of styles and finishes. Anyone experiencing arthritis appreciates the easy-on-the-wrist action.

If implemented as part of the original plan, universal design increases building expenses by no more than 2 to 3 percent. All the materials shown are stock.

Universal design is not only accessible and adaptable, it is affordable and attractive. Incorporating universal design features into your new bathroom ensures a safe environment for you and your family. Being able to negotiate the entrance to a bathroom and close the door is the first major concern. Here are some guidelines:

- The bathroom door must be wide enough for a walker or wheelchair to move through (32 to 36 inches or more).
- Pocket doors that slide into the wall take up less space and may be preferred. Door-opening hardware that does not require finger manipulation is vital.
- Allow a space of at least 5×5 feet to close a conventional door, use fixtures comfortably, and turn a wheelchair 360 degrees.
- Purchase lever-style door handles and fit them on all interior doors.
- Make sure no more than 5 pounds of force is necessary to open doors.

above Doors with lever handles and a width of at least 3 feet make it easy for virtually anyone to enter and leave the bathroom.

mainstreaming UNIVERSAL DESIGN

The seven basic principles of universal design:

- **Equitable use:** Making the design useful and marketable to people with diverse abilities.
- **Flexibility in use:** Accommodating the preferences and abilities of many different people.
- **Simple and intuitive use:** Making the design easy to understand, regardless of the user's experience, knowledge, language skills, or current concentration level.
- **Perceptible information:** Communicating information effectively to the user, regardless of the ambient conditions or the user's sensory abilities.
- **Tolerance for error:** Minimizing hazards and adverse consequences of accidental or unintended actions.
- **Low physical effort:** Making the design easy and comfortable with minimum fatigue.
- **Size and space for approach and use:** Providing appropriate size and space for approach, reach, manipulation, and use, regardless of the user's body size, posture, or mobility.

above Access to this bathroom fits minimum standards for universal design. The tub is low enough to easily navigate and the shower controls are within convenient reach.

Tub and Shower Requirements

- Grab bars are a safety feature in and around the shower and bathtub, making transferring into and out of the tub/shower easier for someone with reduced mobility or strength.
- Bathtub lifts, which lift a person safely into the tub, are available through catalogs, the Internet, and medical supply stores.
- A well-designed bathing space allows standing, sitting, or reclining. An ample shower is typically 36×60 inches.
- To allow for maneuvering in and out of the shower or tub, maintain an open space of at least 18 inches on either side.
- Include a 30-inch-wide aisle along the side of the tub. A wall-mounted sink may be included in this area, but a toilet is not advisable.
- For a shower, allow a 30×48-inch floor space in front for maneuvering.
- Apply antislip rubber pieces to the shower or tub floor.
- For a no-hassle entry, buy or install a shower with a curbless roll-in or no-step entrance.
- Install a fold-down or fixed seat/bench in the tub/shower.
- Install easy-to-turn (without gripping) tub and shower controls. Place them so they can be reached from both inside and outside the tub/shower.
- Consider an adjustable-height showerhead or a handheld showerhead with a 60-inch hose.
- A recessed drain prevents overflowing.
- To prevent burning and to regulate pressure and temperature, attach antiscald devices to all water valves.

left A sliding-bar showerhead adapts to family members of different heights. The tub controls are positioned toward the outside of the tub so that anyone adjusting temperature avoids putting hands under hot running water.

left Dimples on the showerhead handle make it easy to grab and hold. Soap sits on an easy-to-locate platform attached to the shower bar.

Easy-Access Vanity

Sink and Fixture Requirements

Without proper access to sinks, showers, and toilets, daily grooming tasks become difficult. Following are guidelines that will make sinks and fixtures easy to reach and to use.

- Allow a clearance space of 30×48 inches in front of all fixtures.
- It is advisable to install antiscald devices on all water valves. These important devices prevent burning by turning off the water if the temperature gets too hot.
- Mount the sink with the edge no higher than 34 inches. Or install dual-height sinks, one for seated users (32 inches) and one for standing use (36 inches).
- Make sure at least one sink provides clear knee space that measures at least 27 inches high, 30 inches wide, and 19 inches deep. This is also comparative to a vanity-type style of sink. A wall-mounted or pedestal sink is another option.
- Purchase shallow sink basins with overflow at the back to suit those who prefer to sit while using them or to allow children to use a step stool easily.
- Install levers/handles that are easy to grasp with a closed fist.
- Insulate the bottom of the sink and the water pipes to prevent users from getting burns and/or cuts.
- Consider a childproof medicine chest with interior lighting at counter level (minimum of 32 inches) next to the sink.

above This bathroom contains several invisible elements that meet the requirements of universal design, including easy access under the vanity sink. The walls have been reinforced for installation of grab bars. Planning ahead during the construction process will save time and money later.

above and right These photographs show two options for dealing with wheelchair access to the lavatory. *Above,* the cabinet doors under the sink open fully to reveal plenty of knee space. *Right,* open access with no obstructions at all.

Toilet Requirements

above and right Grab-bar reinforcing is installed in the wall when the bathroom is built. This allows easy installation if grab bars are required later by a family member.

Toilet Clearances

When installing a toilet consider these guidelines.

- Allow at least 3×5 feet for approach space.
- Raise toilet height to 17 or 18 inches to prevent unnecessary stress on legs, knees, and back.
- Electronically adjustable seats that raise and lower also are available.
- Install grab bars behind and to the sides of the toilet to assist in standing.
- Removable armrests also assist in standing.

left An adjustable makeup mirror and toiletries tray swing to the front for use. Their contemporary look adds to the bath's clean style.

get a grip on
GRAB BARS

A grab bar is a secure rod used to help lift, steady, balance, or prevent falls. In the bathroom, grab bars aid in the transfer process of getting out of a wheelchair and to the toilet or into the shower or tub. The bars come in a variety of colors and finishes to complement your bathroom motif, although grab bars in contrasting colors enhance visibility.

There are three different types of grab bars:

- Wall-mounted bars are the most stable. You attach them to the wall at both ends and position them vertically or horizontally. Make sure the bar is mounted securely into wall studs or blocking in the walls.
- Pivoting grab bars move out of the way when not in use but are close enough to provide support when needed.
- Sheltering-arm grab bars are on both sides of the toilet providing support similar to the armrest of a chair. This type of grab bar is ideal for older adults when getting up from and sitting down on the toilet.

Grab bars, when mounted properly, bear up to 250 pounds, have no sharp corners or edges, and have non-slip surfaces for easy gripping.

above The Arts and Crafts light fixture is in keeping with the overall decor of the house.

right Natural light accentuates sculptural detailing and warmth in this wicker storage piece.

Lighting

Adequate lighting in any bathroom is important, and it's essential when applying the principles of universal design. Following are guidelines for successful installation.

The bath's lighting scheme needs to include a mix of ambient lighting for overall room illumination, task lighting for concentrated illumination, and accent lighting for displayed art. Other guidelines ensure safety and convenience:

- Mount light switches 44 to 48 inches above the floor.
- To reduce bending, place electrical outlets 18 to 24 inches above the floor (and away from any water sources).
- Light switches that move up and down are easier to turn on and off.

- Install glowing light switches; you can see them in the dark of night.
- Reduce glare with shades, blinds, other window treatments, textured wallpaper, or flat wall paint.
- Consider installing a bathroom phone that provides both light and sound signals on an accessible wall.

Flooring

The flooring in a bathroom must be safe to walk on, easy to maintain, and resistant to damage from water and other spills. Installing nonskid materials or rubber safety strips in the bathing/shower area is highly recommended.

Bathroom floor surfaces should not impede movement of wheels but should not be slippery either. Users are less likely to slip on matte ceramic tiles. Some people prefer a more resilient surface, such as carpet. The best carpet for a bathroom is made of antimicrobial nylon.

In areas that may be potentially slippery or wet, apply antislip rubber decals.

left Stone tiles work well in bathrooms because they don't become slippery when wet. If properly sealed, they will last indefinitely.

Details

Accessorizing in the world of universal design offers the same range of products and accents as other design solutions. After a little research you'll find there are many attractive options.

right The wallpaper pattern contrasts with the stone tiles in the shower, making it easy to see the transition.

far right Towels hang on two bars. The lower one is convenient for children or a person using a wheelchair.

STORAGE ideas

- Vary cabinet storage heights for use by family members with different needs.
- Use lowered wall cabinets or pull-down storage units so that objects and supplies are within range of universal reach requirements (15 to 48 inches).
- Consider cabinet doors that slide horizontally.
- Install light touch magnetic latches on cabinets to allow for easier closure.
- For a linen closet, consider a pocket door with easy-to-grasp hardware.
- Consider loop handles on cabinet doors and drawers.
- Use adjustable shelves on the wall or in the linen closet.

right Brushed nickel fixtures are warm and traditional. The handles are thick and easy to grasp.

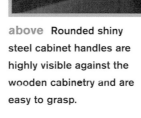

above Rounded shiny steel cabinet handles are highly visible against the wooden cabinetry and are easy to grasp.

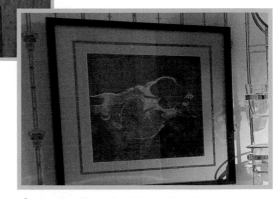

above Use framed paintings, drawings, or posters to add variety and color to the bathroom walls.

Remodeling Diaries

Bathroom remodeling projects vary greatly in cost and complexity. Follow three homeowners as they redo their bathrooms to improve their quality of life while sticking to a budget.

Three homeowners, three budgets, three sets of challenges as each family begins the process of remodeling their bathrooms. Bathrooms are one of the most commonly renovated spaces in the home. With the aid of a day-to-day diary and timelines, this chapter tracks the phases of each remodel and examines the five major stages of a project: Planning, Demolition, Roughing-In the Space, Installation, and Finishing Touches. The three remodels in this chapter represent a common range of budgets and challenges.

Becky Porto set a budget goal of under $4,000 for a small project. Karen and James Peterson decided to commit to an update in the range of $8,000 to $10,000. Reed and Marty Polzin were ready for a complete soup to nuts upgrade and wanted the final figures to come in between $15,000 and $18,000. Each family faced challenges along the way but ended up with bathrooms that more than satisfied their needs.

CHAPTER 7 CONTENTS

left Getting from a boring before to an elegant after requires attention to detail. Each step of the process is equally important and must be completed correctly to guarantee a beautiful and functional bathroom.

Remodeling a Small Bathroom

Week 1: Assessment of Existing Bathroom

Becky Porto originally intended to replace only the dated carpet in her master bathroom. Replacing the carpet with more stylish and durable tiles meant removing the toilet. She decided that because the toilet would be removed anyway, it made sense to replace it with a new model. When visiting the home center she saw a toilet that features a slightly higher seat than standard toilets. Because the homeowner has problems with her knees and hips, the higher toilet was a perfect choice.

BEFORE

left This master bathroom has limited floor space. As she finalized her update Becky made careful choices about the profiles and sizes of the sink and toilet in order to make the room feel more spacious.

below The goal of having updated, durable flooring for the master bath kicked off this entire remodeling project.

above Grouting the tile. Tile is a natural choice for a bathroom floor since it's durable and water-resistant.

PLANNING

REMODELING TIMELINE

WEEK 1 (10/15-10/19)

This timeline provides a quick overview of the Porto remodeling project from the planning stage, measured in weeks, through the entire installation, measured in actual workdays on site. For an in-depth look at the process, read the detailed diary above.

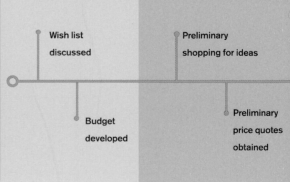

Wish list discussed

Preliminary shopping for ideas

Budget developed

Preliminary price quotes obtained

---

164 Bathroom Design and Planning

Week 2: Making Additional Choices

Once the homeowner had selected the new toilet, she reassessed what she wanted to include in the overall project. Since the bathroom is small, the toilet and sink are in close proximity. Leaving a dated sink next to a new toilet didn't make sense, so Becky began to research sink options. She originally wanted a sink with a base cabinet to gain some additional storage space. Once she looked at how narrow the cabinet would have to be to fit in the bathroom, she realized that the storage space would be filled with plumbing. At that point, she recognized that a pedestal sink was the best option for the space.

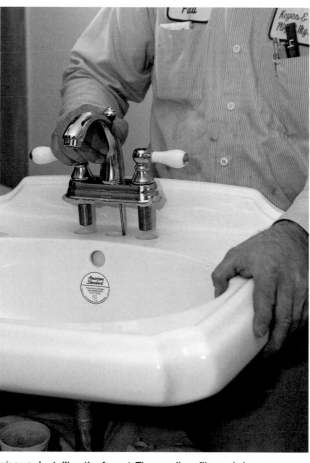

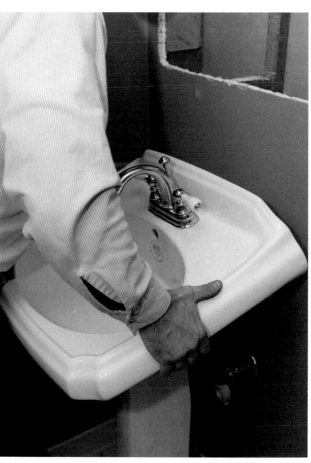

above **Installing the faucet. The small profile, and chrome and porcelain finish of the faucet make it a perfect choice for this bathroom.**

above **Installing the sink. A pedestal sink fits beautifully in a small bathroom such as this.**

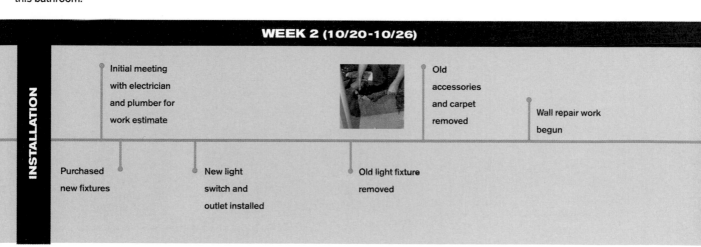

WEEK 2 (10/20–10/26)

INSTALLATION

Initial meeting with electrician and plumber for work estimate

Old accessories and carpet removed

Wall repair work begun

Purchased new fixtures

New light switch and outlet installed

Old light fixture removed

Week 3: Further Selections

As Becky looked at pedestal sinks, she found a style with a small raised backsplash that prevents water from running down the back of the sink. The old vanity light fixture contained only two bulbs and was very narrow, which meant it cast shadows on the mirror. To replace it, she found a slim profile fixture with three bulbs that span the width of the mirror, providing ample light and eliminating the shadows.

After looking at numerous possibilities for a new medicine cabinet/vanity mirror, she realized that it was difficult to find a new one that would fit the small space. Opting for a larger one would have meant removing a stud and rerunning the electrical—work that would have significantly increased the cost of the project. After she selected the new chrome fixtures and accessories for her bath, the decision to keep the existing mirror was sealed because its chrome frame matches the new accessories.

To stay within her budget, Becky knew she couldn't redo the entire bath. She assessed the existing shower and determined that the neutral-color tiles were in great shape and blended well with the new items she had chosen for the bath.

above A new three-bulb light fixture above the vanity bathes the mirror in light, eliminating the harsh shadows cast by the old, smaller fixture. The chrome and porcelain finish on the fixtures and accessories ties the room together.

above Replacing the medicine cabinet. The homeowner decided to keep the existing cabinet because its size and shape were difficult to match. Replacing it with a different cabinet would have increased expenses for removing a stud and rerouting electrical.

WEEK 3 (10/27-11/2)

Wall repairs completed	Floor damage repaired and floor leveled	Tile base installed and tile set
Texture primer applied to walls	Walls and ceilings painted	Floor grouted / Purchased new fixtures

Reality Check

Becky is thrilled with the results of the remodeling project. She laughs when she admits that her favorite part is the new higher profile toilet since it doesn't take a toll on her knees and hips. But she is quick to add that the entire bathroom feels like a brand new space thanks to careful choices of items proportioned to fit into the room without making it feel crowded.

AFTER

The Final Numbers: $3,306

Becky Porto originally planned to replace only the flooring. Once she decided to do a more complete remodeling, her budget goal was between $3,000 and $4,000. By making careful selections about what was remodeled in the room, she was able to stay within her original budget. Here is how the budget broke down:

Fixtures:

- **Tile:** The entire project began with the homeowner's desire to have the old carpet removed and new flooring installed. Because the bathroom is small and the shower remained as-is, the number of tiles needed for the project was minimal. **Price: $103**
- **Toilet:** The homeowner selected a toilet with a slightly higher than standard seat to accommodate her bad knees and hips. **Price: $165**
- **Pedestal sink:** A new pedestal sink complements the updated style of the new toilet. **Price: $169**
- **Sink and shower faucets and fixtures:** The new sink required an updated faucet. Even though the shower stall remained as-is, new shower fixtures update the compartment. **Price: $160**
- **Hardware:** New cabinet door pulls, towel ring, robe hook, and toilet paper holder provide the finishing touches for the updated room at minimal cost. **Price: $60**

Labor and Materials:

- **Electrical:** The homeowner had a new light fixture and switch plates installed. **Price: $236**
- **Plumbing:** Installation included the shower fixtures, sink, and toilet. **Price: $1,393**
- **Repair and finish work: Price: $500**
- **Flooring Installation: Price: $300**
- **Painting:** Included supplies and labor. **Price: $220**

WEEK 4 (11/3-11/9)   **REMODEL FINISHED (11/9)**

Final plumbing fixtures set

New window treatment installed

New light fixture installed

Shopping for new bath accessories

Medicine cabinet installed

Project finished

Remodeling a Mid-sized Bathroom

Assessment of Existing Bathroom

Karen and James Peterson started thinking about remodeling their bathroom for two reasons: the old wallpaper was drab and peeling, and the carpeted floor, though warm underfoot, was difficult to keep clean. Initially the couple considered limiting their project to the floor and walls. But soon they were exploring possibilities for a larger remodeling project. The Petersons reasoned that if they were going to update the bathroom at all, it made sense to do as much as their budget would allow. This would give them a bathroom they could live with for years to come. They settled on a budget of between $8,000 and $10,000 for the complete project. Then they started researching how to get the greatest impact for their money. Karen and James hoped their budget would cover the following items:

- Vanity cabinet
- Countertop
- Toilet
- Light fixtures
- Shower surround
- Sink
- Flooring
- Whirlpool tub
- Faucet
- Paint
- Exhaust fan
- Mirror
- Accessories

BEFORE

left The desire for a more bath-friendly flooring surface helped kick off this remodeling project. Although the homeowners liked the warmth of carpet underfoot, it was difficult to maintain in the moist bath area.

REMODELING TIMELINE

PLANNING

This timeline provides a brief overview of the process the Petersons went through to remodel their bathroom. For a more complete description of the process, read through the diary above.

WEEK 1 (10/15-10-19)

Discussed goals for project

Shopped for ideas

Preliminary price quotes obtained

Measured existing bathroom

Compared samples at home

Making Preliminary Choices

Although a $10,000 budget may seem large, the labor needed to remodel a bathroom is expensive, and costs can quickly add up. Karen and James knew that in order to make all the changes they wanted in their new bath, they would have to be careful selecting fixtures. By choosing an in-stock white toilet and whirlpool tub, in standard sizes, the couple minimized the overall time and cost of the project. Standard, in-stock fixtures are also less expensive than custom sizes and colors, so the Petersons were able to buy more for their money. Clean, white fixtures look fresh and current for years and save homeowners the major expense of replacing outdated colors in the future. If the Petersons eventually want to update their bathroom again, all they'll need is a fresh coat of paint, a new shower curtain, and accessories.

below Installing the tub. A mortar base is installed before setting the whirlpool tub in place. It creates a stable foundation that prevents the tub or shower from shifting.

above Removing the toilet. After turning off the water supply to the toilet, the tank is emptied and removed. Upgrading a toilet is relatively inexpensive and toilets often have to be removed anyway to replace flooring or to make room for a new tub installation. For these reasons, consider a new toilet when planning a bath remodeling project.

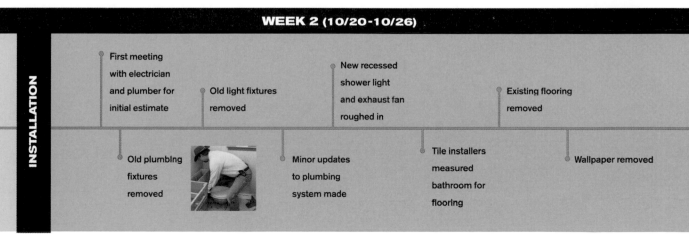

WEEK 2 (10/20-10/26)

INSTALLATION

First meeting with electrician and plumber for initial estimate

Old plumbing fixtures removed

Old light fixtures removed

Minor updates to plumbing system made

New recessed shower light and exhaust fan roughed in

Tile installers measured bathroom for flooring

Existing flooring removed

Wallpaper removed

Remaining Flexible

Midway through the Petersons' bath project, the couple learned that the countertop and tub surround they had chosen were backordered and would take from four to six weeks to arrive. Karen and James were anxious to complete their bath in a timely fashion—they were showering in a cold basement during the job. They opted to choose an alternative solid-surfacing countertop and coordinating tub surround. The new fixtures kept them within their budget and fit the original remodeling timeline. Because the new countertop and surround fit well with the couple's original design, this was a relatively easy switch to make. Typically, a change of plans midway through a project means additional time and money. For the Petersons, making a switch midproject actually saved time.

below Leveling the tub. Before the tub is fastened into place, the installer checks to make sure it is level.

above Wiring the light fixture. A new vanity light scaled to fit the bath is a welcome change from the old oversized light fixtures.

WEEK 3 (10/27-11/2)

Whirlpool tub installed

Switched tub surround and countertop selections

Learned tub surround and countertop were backordered

Walls and ceilings repaired

Researching for Quality

Before choosing fixtures, Karen and James spent time talking about options with the home center's bathroom expert. The couple felt they lacked the technical knowledge to make the best choices without an expert's insight. She assisted them in making top-quality selections for the faucets and shower fixtures. She also helped them select an alternative to their original choice for the vanity countertop. They chose a durable solid surfacing with an integral sink. Karen feels it's a beautiful and practical choice. With no seams to catch dirt, the sink makes it a snap to keep the countertop clean; water just wipes off into the basin.

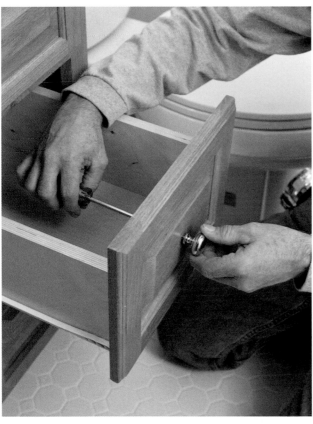

above Attaching new hardware. Simple chrome drawer pulls replace oversized knobs and contribute to the updated style of this bath. Replacing cabinet hardware is an easy and inexpensive way to change the look of a room.

above Painting the cabinets and trim. To stay within the project budget, the homeowners kept the existing built-in cabinetry and woodwork. With a fresh coat of white paint, the bath looks brighter and the cabinets look new.

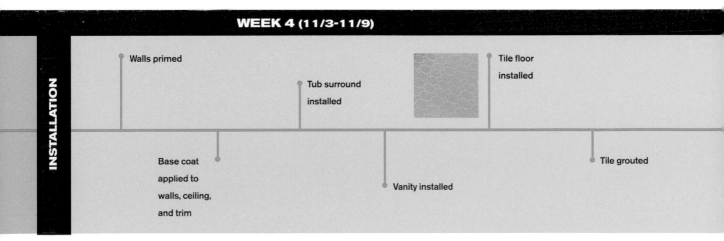

WEEK 4 (11/3-11/9)

INSTALLATION

Walls primed

Tub surround installed

Tile floor installed

Base coat applied to walls, ceiling, and trim

Vanity installed

Tile grouted

Pulling the Look Together

A love of color is seen everywhere in the Petersons' home. Although the couple chose a subdued palette for their new bathroom, they dressed it up in rich washes of color inspired by a new fabric shower curtain. After purchasing the shower curtain, the Petersons selected paint chip samples to match pigments in the fabric. Soon they agreed on a soothing pale green finish for the walls. The new chrome faucets, shower hand sprayer, and cabinet hardware were a natural choice to accentuate the fresh look of the room. Towels, soaps, and other bath accessories pick up additional colors in the shower curtain and pop out against the white backdrop of the countertop, whirlpool, and tub surround.

above Installing the towel bar. New accessories, including updated towel bars and a toilet paper holder put the finishing touches on this bathroom remodeling project.

above The Petersons selected the shower curtain first and used it for inspiration in making selections for the rest of the bathroom.

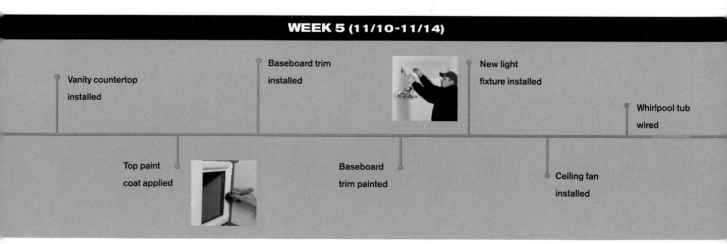

WEEK 5 (11/10-11/14)

Vanity countertop installed

Baseboard trim installed

New light fixture installed

Whirlpool tub wired

Top paint coat applied

Baseboard trim painted

Ceiling fan installed

Reality Check

The Petersons are glad they decided to completely remodel their bathroom rather than limit the work to a new floor and wall finish. The couple recommends fitting as much as possible into a remodeling project. Karen and James took time to research their options before starting and to plan their budget at home before shopping. They realized that costs add up quickly and budgeting helps keep them in hand. Finalizing choices before the remodeling began also minimized costly delays due to changes in plans. The Petersons are comfortable that they got the best possible value for the money they invested in their bathroom.

AFTER

The Final Numbers: $8,786

Karen and James Peterson wanted to include everything they could afford in their bathroom remodeling project without exceeding their budget. As the Petersons made choices about the new fixtures in their bathroom, they kept costs in mind. Here is how the budget broke down:

Fixtures and Appliances:

■ **Flooring:** The homeowners wanted a flooring surface that would be more durable and easier to clean. Tile was an easy choice. **Price: $130**

■ **Electrical:** The addition of an exhaust fan provides the necessary ventilation to keep the updated bath in good shape for years. New vanity lights and a switch plate complete the new lighting scheme. **Price: $185**

■ **Toilet:** The new toilet coordinates with the new vanity and whirlpool tub. **Price: $219**

■ **Whirlpool:** The 5-foot whirlpool tub tucked nicely into the existing tub space. **Price: $700**

■ **Faucets:** Chrome faucets and tub fixtures pull together the overall look of the bath. **Price: $250**

■ **Vanity, countertop, integral sink and hardware:** Because the Petersons kept the same layout in the bathroom to minimize remodeling costs, they selected a new vanity, sink, and countertop that fit in the long, narrow room. **Price: $2,590**

Labor and Materials:

■ **Electrical:** The homeowners had a new light fixture and switch plates installed. **Price: $236**

■ **Plumbing:** Installation included the shower fixtures, sink, and toilet. **Price: $1,393**

■ **Repair and finish work: Price: $500**

■ **Flooring Installation: Price: $300**

■ **Painting:** Included supplies and labor. **Price: $220**

WEEK 5 (11/10-11/14)　　　　　　　　　　　**REMODELING FINISHED (11/14)**

Final plumbing fixtures set

Accessories installed

Cabinet hardware installed

Project finished

Remodeling a Large Bathroom

Planning

Week 1: Assessment of Existing Bathroom

Reed and Marty Polzin assessed their existing family bath and considered features that would best accommodate their busy lifestyle. They developed their wish list by working through checklists similar to the ones suggested in Chapter 3.

After reviewing their initial wish list, the couple decided they wanted an extensive cosmetic remodeling, including new:

- Cabinets
- Countertop
- Toilet
- Tub
- Shower
- Sink and faucet
- Flooring
- Light fixtures
- Paint
- Window treatments
- Mirrors
- Accessories

After deciding what they wanted, they measured the existing space, a smart step to take before meeting with a design professional. (See Chapter 3 for instructions on drawing floor plans and elevation views.)

Reed and Marty developed a preliminary plan and budget and decided to hire professionals to complete the job rather than doing the work themselves. After considering the various types of professionals and the extent of the remodeling job, they decided to work with a general contractor and a certified kitchen and bath designer. The family had budgeted between $15,000 and $18,000 for the work. The actual cost, including some unplanned upgrades, was $20,700.

BEFORE

PLANNING

REMODELING TIMELINE

This timeline provides a quick overview of the Polzins' remodeling project from the planning stage, which is measured in weeks, through the entire installation, which is measured in actual workdays on site. For a more in-depth examination of the process, read through the detailed diary above.

WEEK 1 (2/2-2/8)

Wish list made

Preliminary plan and budget developed

WEEK 2 (2/9-2/15)

Bathroom designer chosen

Initial meetings with plumber, electrician, and plasterer

Week 2: Making Preliminary Choices

"When people are tackling a remodeling project, I encourage them to review the existing space and develop a list of likes and dislikes, then prioritize what they want. Once they determine a budget, we can start reviewing options for materials. Then we can draw up plans and spend some time with them."
—Beth Loerke,
Bathroom Designer

In their first meeting, bathroom designer Beth Loerke helped the homeowners develop several floor plans. Everyone began to review fixtures, materials, and color options for all planned elements of the remodeling project.

Reed and Marty took catalogs and samples home to review, along with the various floor plan options.

The Polzins had preliminary meetings with the plumber, electrician, and plasterer. These professionals were able to provide some useful suggestions, but they were not yet able to provide accurate quotes because many details in the remodeling plan had not been finalized.

The toilet caused much discussion. The homeowners wanted a floor-mounted toilet to replace the existing wall-mounted model but needed to know if the change would be significantly expensive.

Reed and Marty selected a solid-surfacing top with a backsplash and two integrated sinks, making the large countertop area the starting point of their design scheme.

The Polzins walk the aisles of their local Home Depot researching fixtures, materials, and color options for their new bathroom.

WEEK 3 (2/16–2/22)		WEEK 4 (2/23–3/1)			WEEK 5 (3/2–3/8)
	Finalize cost estimates with designer	Tub/shower combination chosen		Switched to whirlpool tub	Design and schedule adjusted for whirlpool tub
Bathroom layout chosen			Obtained painting bid		
	Most materials chosen	Plumber consulted on change to floor-mounted toilet	Light fixtures, combination heater, and paint selected		Project schedule set

Week 3: Selecting More Materials

The couple chose a final layout and figured cost estimates for most of the materials during a second meeting with their designer. They finalized countertops and selected surface materials for the bench seat, a tub/shower combination unit, a neoangle shower, a toilet, and tile for the floor. They also chose some of the paint colors. Decisions were still needed on hardware, accessories, faucets, light fixtures, and window treatments.

doing homework **PAYS OFF**

When Reed and Marty took preliminary measurements of the bath, they discovered that both entryways to the room were only 24 inches wide, and enlarging them was not an option. From the beginning they knew they needed to select fixtures that could be maneuvered into the room.

The existing bath had a window ledge that the homeowners hoped to turn into storage. During consultations with their general contractor, they discovered that the window ledge concealed roof supports. That meant that creating storage would require extensive renovation. At the contractor's suggestion, the homeowners decided to lower the ledge and create a window seat.

DEMOLITION	WORKDAY 1 (3/13)	WORKDAY 2 (3/14)	WORKDAY 3 (3/17)
	Old fixtures, shower enclosure removed	Toilet drain fixed–pitch running wrong way	Lowered window ledge and walls around tub
	Water lines capped	Installed drain lines for new tub	Door trim and old shower wall removed

Week 4: Finalizing the Design

To finalize their budget, the homeowners met with plumber Paul Keyes to confirm their plumbing fixture selections. They were pleased to learn that switching from

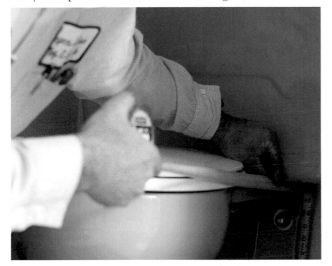

a wall-mounted toilet to a floor-mounted toilet would not significantly add to their budget.

Keyes suggested a whirlpool tub instead of a tub/shower combination. Adding a whirlpool would open the space and prove a nice amenity. The homeowners considered the suggestion but still preferred the tub/shower combination.

The Polzins ordered the cabinets and countertops they had selected the previous week.

After additional time reviewing options, the couple selected mirrors; hardware; faucets; accessories; paint colors; light fixtures; and a combination heater, vent/fan, and light. They ordered the items not in stock.

The Polzins visited a flooring store to review options and to obtain an estimate for the flooring and surrounds. They then chose tile flooring.

They also met with a painter and obtained a bid for painting the ceiling and walls, including a faux finish.

Week 5: Communicating for Great Results

Reed and Marty met with the plumber, electrician, and plasterer to finalize plans and set the schedule. The plumber again suggested that the tub/shower be changed to a whirlpool tub. Now that the couple had selected a larger neoangle shower, they decided to follow the plumber's advice.

As often happens in renovations, one seemingly minor change can have a ripple effect:

- Installing a whirlpool required additional moving of vents and pipes by the plumber.
- The shower wall could be lowered because there would be no shower/tub combination.
- The original plans had called for a light fixture on that same wall. Lowering the wall

eliminated the fixture.
- After deciding to lower the wall by the whirlpool, the homeowners decided to lower the wall next to the toilet as well.
- Light switches needed to be relocated. The electrician recommended installing recessed lighting above the toilet, whirlpool tub, and vanity area. He also suggested moving all the light switches to the wall next to the door. The Polzins agreed to all of these suggestions.

below Lowering the existing window ledge and turning it into a window seat proved a successful design compromise.

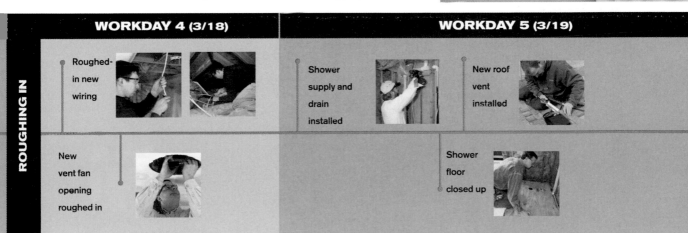

ROUGHING IN

WORKDAY 4 (3/18)

Roughed-in new wiring

New vent fan opening roughed in

WORKDAY 5 (3/19)

Shower supply and drain installed

New roof vent installed

Shower floor closed up

Demolition: Workdays 1–3

Workdays 1–2

Demolition began. The plumber began removing old bathroom fixtures, the shower enclosure, trim, and the vanity and capping off water lines. On Day 2, however, the plumber discovered that the pitch for the toilet drain was running the wrong way and could create backup problems. The homeowners agreed to the additional costs to fix the drain. Once that issue was resolved, the plumber continued removing old materials and installing vents and plumbing.

"Initially we thought it might be cheaper to replace the wall-hung toilet even though we wanted a floor-mount. When we discovered wall-hung models were hard to find and conversion to a floor-mount was only about $100, we decided to go with the conversion. Having the pitch on the drain fixed seemed like the right thing to do."

—Reed Polzin, Homeowner

Reviewing the pitch problem with the old drain, which proves that you never know what you'll find when you open a wall or floor.

Cutting shower enclosure into manageable pieces. Removing the shower enclosure proved to be difficult and time-consuming.

Workday 3

Contractor Rick Nadke lowered the window ledge and the walls around the tub and next to the toilet. He also removed the door trim and the remaining baseboard. Other than drywall installation, demolition is the messiest part of a remodeling job. Plans need to be made to hold debris and for safe disposal of old materials.

The plumber and the contractor worked together during demolition.

"As for the demolition, everything went pretty smoothly. The room was properly prepped and the mess was contained."

—Rick Nadke, Contractor

Removing the old shower wall and exposing wiring.

Lowering the window ledge to window seat height.

WORKDAY 6 (3/20)

Electrical work approved by inspector

Measurements taken for tile floor

Homeowners learn shower base is on back order and that shower doors have been discontinued

Whirlpool set, leveled, and enclosed

Plumber installs supply for tub

Roughing-In: Workdays 4-6

Workday 4

The electricians roughed-in new wiring runs, but did not power up the new cables for outlets, the heater and fan, and the recessed lighting.

During the rough-in, the electrician discovered that the old vent fan did not vent properly to the outside, which code required. Running a new vent to the outside would require additional work and time and a trip to the roof.

Installing wall outlets and switches.

Roughing-in the vent opening.

Workday 5

The contractor continued to rebuild the walls that would enclose the shower. He also closed up the shower floor after

Installing insulation before putting moisture barrier in.

Enclosing the shower drain.

the plumber installed the drain and supply assemblies for the shower.

A sheet metal professional came in to install the new vent fan to the roof. This involved running a duct to the roof, cutting an opening in the roof, and installing a vent cap. Preventing leaks with proper flashing and sealants on the roof is essential.

The electrical inspector was due on-site the next day to review the work.

Workday 6

The homeowners decided on another change: a whirlpool with its own hot-water heater. The plumber returned to set the new tub and the drain for the shower. The contractor installed the knee wall for the tub. While measuring the floor and surrounds, installers recommended removing the old floor to ensure greater stability for the new tile.

The electrical inspector approved the electrical work done to date.

Several unexpected challenges cropped up on this day.

- The homeowners learned that the shower base they had selected was on back order. They decided to go with a tile shower base rather than waiting.
- The chosen white shower doors had been discontinued. The Polzins decided to order a silver door that could be delivered quickly.
- The original tub plan called for a single 20-amp/120-volt circuit. With the final decision to install a heated whirlpool, the electrician needed to add an additional 20-amp/120-volt GFCI circuit after the electrical rough in was completed.

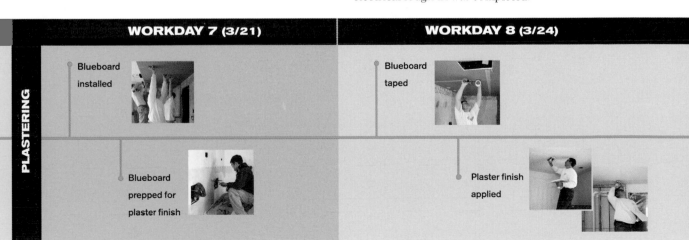

WORKDAY 7 (3/21)	WORKDAY 8 (3/24)
Blueboard installed	Blueboard taped
Blueboard prepped for plaster finish	Plaster finish applied

PLASTERING

Plastering: Workdays 7–8

Workdays 7–8

The Polzins considered patching the drywall, but there was a significant amount of damage from the roughing-in for the vent opening. The couple decided to hang new blueboard on the ceiling and to install blueboard on the walls. A plaster coating would be skimmed later.

"Because they needed to patch so many areas of the wall after the removal of the tub, shower, and toilet, we felt it would be cost-effective to replaster the whole room rather than trying to match the existing walls. Also, some walls were brought down to open things up, so we wanted to ensure that the room looked clean and consistent. However, we did not use drywall. We used a material called blueboard or plasterboard to get the plaster to bond correctly."

—*Cliff Uitenbroek, Plasterer*

Installing blueboard on ceiling.

Taping ceiling.

Smoothing the plaster coat.

Applying bonding agent to walls prior to plastering.

Applying plaster finish.

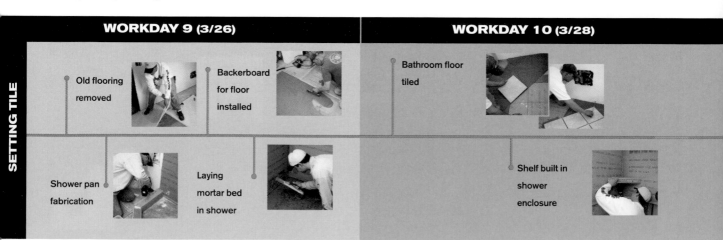

SETTING TILE

WORKDAY 9 (3/26)

Old flooring removed

Backerboard for floor installed

Shower pan fabrication

Laying mortar bed in shower

WORKDAY 10 (3/28)

Bathroom floor tiled

Shelf built in shower enclosure

Setting Tile: Workdays 9–12

Workdays 9–12

Once the walls were finished, the tilers arrived to install the floor, tub, and shower enclosures. The first steps were to remove the old flooring and begin fabricating the shower pan.

After discussions with the tile installers, Reed and Marty realized they could have an even larger shower because the tile pan was being custom-made. After checking prices, a local vendor was located to make custom shower doors at a reasonable price. The homeowners were pleased and

enjoyed the idea of a roomier shower.

Remodeler's Note: In a bathroom installation, work is not done for one fixture or element at a time before moving on to the next, as may happen with other projects. It is more common to do some of the work for all of the fixtures at the same time. For example, it's fairly standard to do the framing at one time, followed by the rough plumbing for all of the fixtures, then the installation of the tile and wallboard, followed by the finish plumbing work.

Removing the old floor.

Putting down backerboard for the floor.

Laying membrane in the shower pan.

Laying mortar in the shower pan.

Tiling the shower enclosure.

Grouting the shower walls and ceiling.

WORKDAY 11 (3/29)

Shower enclosure tiled

WORKDAY 12 (3/30)

Tile on all surfaces grouted

Cleaning up after tiling is completed

Prime, Paint, Install: Workdays 13–16

Workday 13

The walls and ceiling were primed and painted as the contractor set the vanity cabinets and the linen cabinet. Face frames and doors were hung. The painter applied a faux finish to the wall above the space for the vanity, which was set in place.

Priming walls.

Setting vanity in place.

Workday 14

The painter applied the faux finish to the rest of the walls while the contractor finished trim work on the cabinets and hung the soffit for the recessed lighting above the vanity. He also installed the kick plates on the cabinets and added crown molding to the closet.

"I like the sponging technique because you can be as dramatic as you want. You can bring in multiple colors and add some texture to the space. It also tends to hide imperfections. If you need to do any repairs, they don't have to be perfect."

—*Gregg J. Kranzusch, painter*

Sponging on faux finish. The painter added a layer of color with a natural sea sponge.

Installing the lighting soffit above the vanity sinks.

Workday 15

The electricians returned to put in the lights, fan, and outlets while an installer placed and caulked the countertop backsplash. A carpenter took a measurement for the seat on the window bench. The electricians also wired the whirlpool. The bathroom was definitely coming together.

Installing recessed lighting above sinks.

Caulking backsplash for vanity sinks.

Installing and leveling the floor-mounted toilet.

Installing vanity plumbing fixtures.

WORKDAY 13 (4/1)	**WORKDAY 14 (4/3)**
Vanity and linen cabinets set Vanity set in place	Faux finish applied 
Ceiling primed and painted Doors hung	Cabinet trim finished Kickplates and molding installed 

PRIME, PAINT, INSTALL

Workday 16

The plumber returned to install the final fixtures. The contractor installed the cabinet hardware and accessories such as towel bars. The major work was done.

Installing a GFCI outlet above the vanity.

Installing the towel rod above the bathtub.

Installing the showerhead.

MAY I SEE YOUR PERMITS, PLEASE?

Most renovations and additions will require building permits. In many locations, separate permits are issued for the building, plumbing, electrical, and mechanical stages of the renovation. For a project involving minor alterations to your bath, the permit may be issued immediately.

If major structural changes are planned, the building inspection department may need to review the plans before issuing the permit. Your schedule should allow several days for this process. Your contract will probably specify that the contractor is responsible for obtaining all necessary permits, but it is still a good idea to educate yourself on the process and perhaps have a brief meeting with your local building code officials.

"We found that we didn't need a general building permit for the bathroom because we weren't doing any work on load-bearing or exterior walls. We did need to obtain a plumbing and electrical permit from the city. Each of the professionals took care of securing those permits and arranging for the inspector to review and approve the work. The work was approved by a city inspector after the plumbing was roughed in. It is called a rough-in inspection and is complete once all pipes and vents are in place. They are capped off until final installation of fixtures. The same holds true for the electrical work. Once it's roughed in and the wiring is run, the inspection is completed. The work needs to be approved before walls are closed and final fixtures set."

—Rick Nadke, Contractor

WORKDAY 15 (4/7)

Final electrical installed

Whirlpool wired

Measuring for the window seat

WORKDAY 16 (4/8)

Plumbing fixtures installed

Accessories installed

Cabinet hardware installed

Finishing Touches: Workday 17

Workday 17

The bench seat, custom shower doors, and mirrors were installed. Once these items were in place, the bathroom was considered finished and ready for use.

Installing the seat on the bench.

Installing the shower enclosure.

Installing glass shower door.

Installing the vanity mirror.

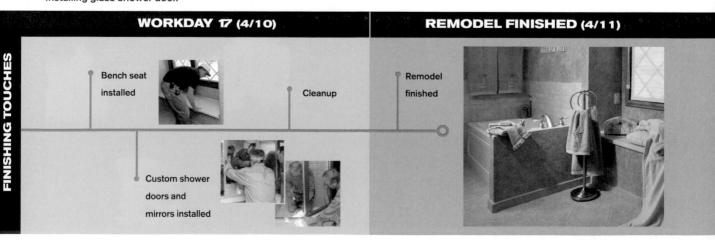

FINISHING TOUCHES

WORKDAY 17 (4/10)

Bench seat installed

Cleanup

Custom shower doors and mirrors installed

REMODEL FINISHED (4/11)

Remodel finished

Reality Check

AFTER

The Pleasures of a New Bathroom

The Polzins' objectives were to make the space more open and to update the room. They also wanted a larger shower, a floor-mounted toilet, and originally wanted a tub/shower combination. Substituting a whirlpool tub gave them everything they wanted and more. Reed likes the larger neoangle shower and the look of the tile. Marty enjoys the whirlpool and the solid-surfacing vanity.

The Polzins say success involves communication of all parties. Each professional must have a clear picture of all elements of the project up front to avoid errors and delays.

AFTER

The Polzins' Final Numbers: $20,700

The original budget goal was between $15,000 and $18,000. Including some unexpected problems and some last-minute upgrades, here is how the Polzins' budget broke down:

Fixtures and Appliances

■ **Cabinets:** The homeowners wanted to get away from the dark, grainy wood that was previously in the room, so they selected a lighter maple. They felt it was rich-looking and chose a simple door style. **Price: $3,000**

■ **Hardware:** They selected satin nickel knobs and pulls for price, style, and coordination with other fixtures. **Price: $250**

■ **Countertop and integral sinks, window seat:** The homeowners liked the look and colors/patterns available in solid-surfacing materials. Also, from a maintenance and cleaning standpoint, they liked the idea of integral sink bowls. **Price: $2,400**

■ **Faucets and accessories:** They selected fixtures in a pearl nickel finish for the look and style of the products. These included towel bars, shower fixtures, tub spout, handles, toilet paper dispenser, and faucets. **Price: $1,000**

■ **Whirlpool:** After changing their minds, the couple selected a whirlpool with a heater. **Price: $750**

■ **Toilet:** A new toilet complements the whirlpool tub. **Price: $200**

■ **Window treatments:** The couple liked the look and function of translucent shades. **Price: $450**

■ **Tile:** Marty and Reed felt the tile would add to the resale value of their home. The tile was also available in various sizes, which allowed coordination between the shower, tub surround, and floor. **Price: $2,000**

■ **Shower doors and mirrors:** Because the couple decided to purchase custom doors, they looked for cost-effective options, keeping the nickel finish of other fixtures in mind. The mirrors were selected by the designer, who wanted something functional and interesting. **Price: $1,000**

Labor and Materials

■ Home center design services:	No charge
■ Contractor/remodeler:	$1,300
■ Plumber:	$4,000
■ Electrician:	$1,500
■ Tile setter:	$2,000
■ Plasterer:	$500
■ Painter:	$350

Contact Information and Resources

Contact Information

The Home Depot® offers bathroom products and materials from major manufacturers either in stock or through special order. This extensive inventory offers customers a comprehensive and varied selection that will ensure a kitchen that truly reflects their personal style, and taste while enabling them to stick to a realistic budget. Information on products and materials can be obtained from design centers in Home Depot stores or directly through manufacturers by mail, telephone, or online.

Contacting Meredith Corporation

To order this and other Meredith Corporation books call 800/678-8091. For further information about the information contained in this book, please contact the manufacturers listed or contact Meredith by e-mail at hi123@mdp.com or by phone at 800/678-2093.

Contacting The Home Depot

For general information about product availability contact your local Home Depot or visit The Home Depot® website at www.homedepot.com

Bathroom Accessories

American Standard
800/442-1902
www.americanstandard-us.com

Häfele Cabinet Accessories
800/667-8721
www.haef.com

Cabinetry and Hardware

American Woodmark
www.woodmark-homedepot.com
service@woodmark.com
540/665-9100

Amerock Corporation
800/435-6959

Berenson Hardware
www.berensonhardware.com

Häfele Cabinet Accessories
800/667-8721
www.haef.com

KraftMaid Cabinetry
15535 South State Ave.
Middlefield, OH 44062
Tel: 800/571-1990
www.kraftmaid.com

Merillat Industries, LLC
800/575-8761
www.merillat.com

Mills Pride
Sold exclusively at The Home Depot®
www.millspride.com

Premier Cabinetry
www.premiercabinetry.com
customer_service@premiercabinetry.com
800/441-0337

Schrock Cabintery
www.schrock.com

Thomasville Cabinetry
www.thomasvillecabinetry.com
thomasville.cabinetry@homedepot.com
800/756-6497

Woodcrafters
800/235-7747 (Florida and Southwest division only)

Countertops

Corian
800/4-CORIAN® (800/426-7426)
www.corian.com

Pionite/Panolam
800/746-6483
www.pionite.com
Countertop—Chile Fiber, Suede (AO101-S)

Silestone by Cosentino
Cosentino USA
281/494-7277
www.silestoneusa.com

U.S. Ceramic Tile Company
www.usctco.com

Wilsonart
www.wilsonart.com

Flooring

Armstrong
www.armstrong.com

Bruce
800/236-2275

E-mail: totalat7359799@aol.com

Echeguren Slate, Inc.
800/992-0701
www.echeguren.com
Slate—Indian Silver Black

Pergo
800/33-PERGO (800/337-3746)
www.pergo.com

Wilsonart
www.wilsonart.com

Lighting

Georgia Lighting
www.georgialighting.com
866/544-4861

Hampton Bay
www.homedepot.com

Progress Lighting
www.homedepot.com

Plumbing and Fixtures

American Standard
800/524-9797 ext. 1007
www.americanstandard-us.com

Delta Faucet Company
www.deltafaucet.com

Eljer Plumbingware
E-mail: contactus@eljer.com
Phone: 877/355-3376
Fax: 877/460-2483

Elkay Sales, Inc.
www.elkayusa.com

Glacier Bay Faucets
Exclusively through The Home Depot®
www.glacierbayfaucets.com

GROHE America, Inc.
630/582-7711
www.groheamerica.com

International Thermocast
Sales Support e-mail:
    sales_support@thermocastsinks.com
Phone: 678/445-2022
Fax: 678/445-2039
www.thermocastsinks.com

Insinkerator
800/558-5712
www.insinkerator.com

Kohler Co.
800/4-KOHLER (800/456-4537)
www.kohler.com

KWC Faucets Inc.
888/592-3287
www.kwcfaucets.com

Pegasus Faucets
www.pegasus.com
www.homedepot.com

Sinks, Showers, Toilets, & Tubs

American Standard
800/442-1902
www.americanstandard-us.com

Corian
800/4-CORIAN®
(800/426-7426)
www.corian.com

Kohler Co.
800/4-KOHLER (800/456-4537)
www.kohler.com

Resources

Product Information

Listed below are the names and manufacturers of many of the products seen throughout the book. To find a product shown in a photograph, locate the product type (resources listed below) and the page number of the photo that interests you. Page numbers are next to manufacturers' names. To determine whether the product you are interested in is available to you, contact the manufacturer. Contact information for each manufacturer follows the resources. Most of the products, or their equivalent, are available through The Home Depot, although there are some items shown that are unique to the photography location and may not be available. If the page number is not listed, no information about that particular product is available.

Colors

Please be aware that paint colors shown in the book may look different on your wall because of the printing process used in this book. If you see a color you like, show it to a Home Depot associate in the paint department, and he or she will custom-tint paint to match it as closely as possible. Buy samples of paint in small quantities and test areas so that you can see the result prior to spending time and money to paint an entire room. Changes in lighting affect colors, which, for instance, can seem remarkably different under artificial light and natural light. Also, consult everyone who will be living with the color. Paint a test area and live with it under different lighting conditions for at least 24 hours to make sure it is right for you.

Contacting Meredith Corporation

For further information, please contact the manufacturers listed or contact Meredith by e-mail at hi123@mdp.com or by phone at 800/678-2093.

T=Top, C=Center, B=Bottom, L=Left, R=Right

Bathroom Accessories: American Standard—18CR, 46, 48, 85C, 120BL, 166-167 ■ **Bath Unlimited**—68-71, 166-167 ■ **Häfele**—154, 158TL, 159BL ■ **Thomasville**— 74-76 (mirror) ■ **Kohler**—50, 123BR

Bidets: Kohler—57L, 67BR, 91, 98BR, 99TL, 99BR, 133TL

Cabinetry: American Standard—134TR ■ **The Home Depot®**—173 (towel bar) ■ **KraftMaid**—22TR, 96TR, 142CL, 143BR, 151BR, ■ **General Marble**—171, 173 ■ **Thomasville**—72-77

Cabinetry Hardware: Amerock—22TR ■ **Häfele**—161CL ■ **Liberty**—74-77, 171, 173

Countertops: Corian—6-7, 21BC, 93BL, 96BL, 122TR, 123TL, 144TC, 173 ■ **Silestone**—23BR, 24-25, 145TR ■ **Wilsonart**—74-77

Flooring and Walls: Corian—173 (shower surround) ■ **Daltile**—46, 48-49, 68-71, 89, 173 ■ **Total Floor Covering**—6-7, 15TR, 21BC, ■ **Topravit LTD.**—72-77 ■ **Thai Ceramic Tile Co.**—164 (floor tiles) ■ **US Ceramic**—50, 52-53, 92, 164 (baseboard tiles)

Lighting: Hampton Bay—166-167, 170, 173 ■ **Light Unlimited**—46, 48-49 ■ **Progress**—50 ■ **Regal King**—68-7, 92

Shower Fixtures: American Standard—49, 32TL, 89, 90TR, 132BL

Delta—172 ■ **Dornbracht**—20TR ■ **Kohler**—50, 72, 76, 89, 90BR-CL, 126TR, 132TR, 132BR, 157 ■ **Moen**—65CL

Shower Exhaust Fans: Broan—46, 173

Shower Pans: American Standard—131TR

Showers: American Standard—101CR, 102BL ■ **Basco**—55, 56BC, ■ **Kohler**—65CL, 104TR, 131BL

Sink Faucets: American Standard—46, 48-49, 84, 120TL, 122CR, 127CR, 165, 166-167 ■ **Delta**—23TL, 40BL, 56, 95TR, 127TR, 153BC ■ **Dornbracht**—16TR ■ **Kohler**—5TL, 5BR, 13TL, 18TL, 41TC, 41TR, 50, 52-53, 62-63, 66BC, 67TC, 68-71, 82, 84BC, 85BR, 86TR (all three), 95BL, 97TR, 100TC, 106TR, 120-121, 123CL, 123BR, 126TL, 127BR, 154-155, 158 ■ **Moen**—40BR ■ **Pegasus**—173

Sinks: American Standard—8TR, 40BR, 41CC, 41CR, 46, 48-49, 84101CR, 120TL, 122CR, 127CR, 134TR, 164-165, 166-167 ■ **Corian**—96BL, 122TR, 123TL, 144TC ■ **Kohler**—5TL, 13TL, 18TL, 41TC, 41TR, 50, 52-53, 56, 62-63, 66BC, 67TC, 68-71, 82, 84BC, 85BR, 95TR, 95BL, 97TR, 100TC, 106TR, 120-121, 123CL, 123BR, 124TL, 124TR, 153CR, 154-155, 158, 161CR

Toilets: Kohler—18TL, 20BR, 50, 53, 57L, 65TR, 68-71, 77, 84BC, 91, 94TR, 97TR, 98TL, 100TC, 133TL, 148CL, 154, 158, 159, 167, 171, 173

Tub Fixtures: Delta—6-7, 21BC ■ **Dornbracht**—126BR ■ **Kohler**—62, 64TR, 153BR

Tubs: American Standard—6-7, 103TL ■ **Kohler**—50, 54, 59BL, 62, 64BL, 65C, 72, 76, 89, 129BL

Acknowledgments

Special Thanks to:
Tom and Lorena Ament
Daniel and Amy Argall
Herb Gama
Mary and Robert Joehnk
Mark and Patricia Kadlec
Karen and James Peterson
Tom and Becky Poehlman
Reed and Marty Polzin
Becky Porto
David and Jane Rivera
Todd and Tammy Sarauer
Anton and Deb Schwarz
Mark and Martha Shultz
Lisa Yetter Ulrich and Bob Ulrich
Ted and Kari Voissem

The Center for Universal Design
North Carolina State University
Campus Box 8613
Raleigh, NC 27695-8613
www.design.ncsu.edu/cud

National Kitchen & Bath Association
687 Willow Grove Street
Hackettstown, NJ 07840
877/NKBA-PRO (877/652-2776)
www.nkba.com

Chapter 2

Pages 26–31
Additional pages—16BR, 17TR, 26–31,
104TL, 129TL, 136TR, 143CC, 146TL,
148–149, 150TR, 151CL, 153BCL
Builder: John Amanson, General
Contractors
San Francisco, California
415/927-8888
E-mail: jamanson@earthlink.net
Design/Installation: Kitchen Studio 150
San Francisco, California
415/864-5093
kitchenstudio150@aol.com

Pages 32–37
Additional pages—1BL, 135TR, 142BR,
144TR, 147TL, 150BC, 153TR
Builder: Thierfelder Builder, Inc.
Bob Thierfelder

Pages 62–67
Additional pages—5TL, 20BR, 84BC,
95BL, 104TR, 129BL, 143TC, 148TL,
150CR, 153BR
Architect: Lindsay Associates Architects
Glenview, Illinois
847/724-8777
Builder: Trustway Homes
Pewaukee, Wisconsin
262/695-6400
www.trustway.com

Pages 68–71
Architect: Jeff Hibbard Design Services,
Inc.   (920) 731-7365
hibbarddesign@aol.com
Builder: Tom Ament
Kaukauna, Wisconsin
(920) 766-7900
tja@wiscobuilds.com
Interior Design: Elite Home Creations
Deb Van Straten
(920) 419-1789
elitehomes@new.rr.com
Interior Decorating: Kathy Mitchell
Menasha, Wisconsin
(920) 729-6006
redesigns@ameritech.net

Additional Photography:
Pages—15BR, 95CR, 124CR, 129BR,
132BR, 143TR, 143CL, 151TR, 152CL,
152BR, 153BCR
Designer: Vogel Design Group
Eric Vogel
Milwaukee, Wisconsin
www.vogeldesigngroup.com

Pages—16TL, 132TR, 146TR
Designer: Robert Guenther
Milwaukee, Wisconsin
414/272-1051

Chapter 6

Pages 154–161
Additional pages—94TR, 100TC,
126TR, 143BC, 146TC
Architect/Project Manager: Rosemann
& Associates, Eddie Tapper
Kansas City, Missouri
816/472-1448
www.rosemann.com
Property Owner/Executive Director:
Universal Design Housing Network
Paul Levy
Kansas City, Missouri
816/751-7898
www.udhn.org
Interior Design: American Society of
Interior Designers, Missouri-West/
Kansas Chapter
Carolyn Wear, ASID
913/268-9126
Doreen Gregory, ASID
913/341-5917
Sallie Kytt Redd, ASID
913/492-3158
Sheryl Koch, ASID
816/537-6364
Kelly Stewart
816/803-0036

Deborah Cook
816/313-8104
Suzette Burton
888/471-1715

Chapter 7

Pages 162–185
Additional pages—6–7, 21BC, 22TR,
131TL, 135BC
Electrical: Team Services
Appleton, Wisconsin
920/738-5885
julief@new.rr.com
Kitchen and Bath Design Center:
Beth Loerke, Home Depot #4903
Painting: Gregg J. Kranzusch Painting
Neenah, Wisconsin
Plastering: Uitenbroek Plastering Inc.
Appleton, Wisconsin
920/749-0787
Plumbing: Keyes & Sons Plumbing
& Heating, Inc.
Appleton, Wisconsin
920/725-2494
Shower doors and mirrors:
Valley Glass Inc.
Appleton, Wisconsin
920/733-4477
Tiling: Total Floor Covering
Appleton, Wisconsin
800/236-2275
totalat7359799@aol.com

Want to do it yourself?

If you're interested in renovating or remodeling your kitchen on your own The Home Depot® 1-2-3 library offers clear and concise step-by-step, project-driven books to help you through the process.

Titles include: *Home Improvement 1-2-3*, *Decorating 1-2-3*, *Decorative Painting 1-2-3*, *Wiring 1-2-3*, *Plumbing 1-2-3*, *Flooring 1-2-3*, and *Tiling 1-2-3*. These books are available at The Home Depot and at bookstores throughout North America

Index